D1565809

BLUE
sparrow

Rediscover the Rosary

Rediscover the Rosary

THE MODERN POWER
OF AN ANCIENT PRAYER

MATTHEW KELLY

BLUE SPARROW
North Palm Beach, Florida

BLUE
sparrow

Rediscover the Rosary

Copyright © 2017 Kakadu, LLC
Published by Blue Sparrow
Blue Sparrow is an imprint of Beacon Publishing, Inc.

Hardcover ISBN: 978-1-929266-50-0
Paperback ISBN: 978-1-929266-51-7
Ebook ISBN: 978-1-929266-52-4
Audiobook ISBN: 978-1-929266-81-4

Design by Madeline Harris

Library of Congress Cataloging-In-Publication Data
Names: Kelly, Matthew, author.
Title: Rediscover the rosary : the modern power of an ancient prayer /
by Matthew Kelly.
Description: North Palm Beach : Beacon Publishing, 2017.
Identifiers: LCCN 2017020576 | ISBN 9781929266500 (hardcover) |
ISBN 9781929266517 (softcover) | ISBN 9781929266524 (e-book) |
ISBN 9781929266814 (audiobook)
Subjects: LCSH: Rosary. | Prayer—Catholic Church. |
Rosaries (Prayer books)
Classification: LCC BX2163 .K394 2017 | DDC
242/.74—dc23

For more information visit:
www.MatthewKelly.com

FIRST EDITION

10   9   8   7   6   5   4   3

Printed in the United States of America

For Father Ron Rieder

Long before it was popular, you recognized that
Dynamic Catholic could be something unique and powerful.
You foresaw the incredible possibilities that would be unleashed
by collaborations between Dynamic Catholic and pastors.

I know you have prayed and suffered unceasingly
for the Dynamic Catholic mission, and for me personally.
May God bless you and reward you a thousand times for your generosity.

Thank you for all your love and support. You will never know how
much your encouragement has meant to me.

For Kathy Aull

For fifteen years you have served me selflessly and lovingly.
Everything you do allows me to do a little bit more of what I do. I
simply could not have done all I have done without your contribution.

So I hope you will see a little bit of yourself and your contribution in
every book, every speech, every program, and everything
Dynamic Catholic has done, is doing, and will do in the future.

Thank you. May your life continue to be filled with love,
laughter, and dreams come true.

• • • • • •

Neither of you will ever know the impact you have had on my
life or on the ministry God has entrusted to me and
to the team at Dynamic Catholic.

I am honored and humbled to know you.

m.

Table of Contents

PROLOGUE   xiii

PART ONE

1. My Journey with the Rosary   1
2. A Unique Perspective   13
3. Praying with Beads   21
4. Dynamic Prayer   35

PART TWO

5. The Joyful Mysteries   61
6. The Luminous Mysteries   83
7. The Sorrowful Mysteries   109
8. The Glorious Mysteries   131

PART THREE

9. A Scriptural Rosary   155

PART FOUR

10. Every Family Needs a Prayerful Giant   207
11. Beautifully Aware   213

APPENDICES

The Basics: How to Pray the Rosary   237
Quotes, Prayers, and Hymns About Mary and the Rosary   247
Marian Feast Days   263

Prologue

A treasure map does not become worthless because it is old. Nobody finds one and throws it away simply because it is aged and worn. Its value is not determined by how new or old it is. The value of a treasure map is determined by two factors: Does the map lead to treasure? How great is the treasure?

Age does not make something less valuable or irrelevant. But that is the foolishness of our era. There is a legendary Australian wine called Grange Hermitage. At about $40,000, a 1951 bottle of Grange Hermitage is certainly not less valuable because it is old. No wine collector in the world would say, "It's no good because it's old."

Every era is arrogant about itself in different ways. The people of this age have a tendency to look down on things that are old, and a particular way of dismissing ancient wisdom as irrelevant to modern life. The Catholic faith and the Rosary have suffered at the hands of this foolishness. Many people, Catholic and not, dismiss Catholicism and its practices such as the Mass and the Rosary as irrelevant and having nothing to offer, simply because they are old. This is one of many forms of blind ignorance that plague our age.

Catholicism is a treasure map. I concede, it is a very old treasure map, but it still leads to treasure—and the treasure is immeasurable. There is no need to apologize for its truth, beauty, and wisdom. Our times lack all three.

The Rosary, in the very same way, is also an ancient treasure map, and it still leads to treasure. It is an inexhaustible treasure trove. Take all you can from it today, and if you return tomorrow, you will discover that the treasures the Rosary has to offer are even greater than yesterday's.

My Journey with the Rosary

I'm a practical man. Anyone who really knows me will tell you this. I like things that work. I've nothing against theories, but I prefer ideas that actually work. People helping other people inspire me. Organizations that add tremendous value to communities inspire me. There's something fabulous about things that work.

We know this best when things stop working. It is amazing how a phone or computer that stops working can turn our lives upside down. We have a habit of appreciating things most when they are gone. When I was really sick, I resolved that I would never take my health for granted again, but of course I do.

And we have this great expectation that things will just work. Sure, there are things that are broken in our country and culture, but even the broken stuff works pretty well. Are health care and education broken? Absolutely, but let's not take for granted the incredible good these systems are doing despite their brokenness. Is our political system in need of a good overhaul? Probably, but we still have remarkable order considering how broken it all seems at this time.

Visit any not so advanced country and you will very quickly realize that there are lots of places in this world where a great many things just don't work. You will most likely leave wondering: *How do people live in these places?*

Perhaps that is why I have a bias toward the practical, a massive bias toward things that actually work. The point is: I like things that work. I love things that work.

People often ask me questions about the Rosary. Do you pray the Rosary? Why? How often? Did you pray it as a child with your family? Does the Rosary really matter? How much? Do Catholics worship Mary? Why do we pray to her?

There are a thousand variations on these questions, but there are three things I always like to tell people in any conversation about the Rosary:

1. It works.
2. It will fill you with an incredible sense of peace.
3. Don't take my word for it.

The Rosary works. There is just something about it that settles our hearts and minds. It puts things in perspective and allows us to see them as they really are. It reaches deep down into our souls and puts us at ease, creating a peace that is rare and beautiful.

How many things can you do that will achieve what I just described? Go back and read that short paragraph one more time. When I say "rare and beautiful," I am not just using words. I very much mean what I say. And it has been my experience that the only people who do not value that kind of peace are those who have never tasted it. If that is you, I am so excited for you. The Rosary is going to change your life.

But here is my challenge: Don't take my word for it. Try it for yourself. Develop a habit of praying the Rosary.

I don't expect that you will pray the Rosary once and say to yourself, "Matthew was absolutely right. Praying the Rosary really works. My heart and mind are settled. Everything is in perspective now! I can see clearly what matters most and what matters least. My soul is at ease, and I have this untouchable deep and abiding peace."

No, it requires a habit. It may be something you pray every Wednesday night. That's how I got started. It may be something you pray on the first Saturday of each month. It may be something you feel called to do every day. We will speak about how often to pray the Rosary, and the seasons of our spiritual lives, a little later. All I want to establish here is that to really experience the tremendous fruits of the Rosary, it has been my experience that you need to establish it as a spiritual habit in your life.

We live hectic lives in a chaotic world. All this can lead to a confusion that fogs the mind, unsettles the soul, and leads to poor decisions. Amid all this chaos and confusion, our souls yearn for peace and clarity. Are you at peace? I'm not. Right now, sitting here writing these lines, but also in my life at the moment, I don't have that peace. I've had a bad day. We all do from time to time. It's been a rough week. The wheels just seem to have fallen off in three or four situations, all at the same time. And it's been a long month. I had to add a couple of trips unexpectedly to my schedule, my wife is seven months pregnant, one of my businesses is in transition, Dynamic Catholic continues to explode in a fabulous way but there are challenges with that, I haven't been exercising, and I catch myself cutting corners in my prayer life.

So, no, I am not really at peace right at the moment. I have fallen into what seems to be a perennial problem for me: overcommitment. When life gets like this I know that some of the things I am busying myself with God doesn't want me doing. Each time it happens I have to humble myself and go back and say to God, "Tell me again what you want me doing right now." This is always a good time to pray the Rosary and allow God to fill me again with peace and clarity.

ARE YOU A GOOD LISTENER?

All prayer is an attempt to speak to and listen to God. But listening is so much more difficult than we think. It requires patience and awareness. Listening to other people is hard enough, but listening to God takes the challenge to a whole new level.

Most people think they are better at listening to others than they are. Research suggests that the average person listens with only 25 percent efficiency. That's a lot we are missing. If I'm an average listener, that means I miss 75 percent of what my wife tells me. It's astounding, really. If you have an adult child and you are an average listener, over the course of a lifetime you've missed three-quarters of what your son or daughter has been trying to say to you. Even if you are twice as good at listening than the average listener, you've still missed half of what your child has been trying to share with you. No wonder we have misunderstandings and disagreements.

If you want to be a better listener, I could tell you: Be empathetic, eliminate distractions so that you are present, remember that you are not perfect, ask questions to gain further insight, don't run from being uncomfortable, don't change the subject, try not to be judgmental, don't interrupt, and pause before responding. But what it all comes down to is getting out of your own way.

Why are most people such poor listeners? What is the key to becoming a great listener? The answers to both of these questions are linked.

We get in the way. We think about ourselves, rather than thinking about the person speaking. We get absorbed in how what is being said relates to us, rather than trying to work out how it relates to the person we are listening to. When we are preoccupied with ourselves, we cannot hear what others are trying to say to us. When we are able to set our own needs aside and focus on the other person, our listening skills increase exponentially.

Listening to others is difficult; listening to God is even harder. Many things get in the way of hearing other people, and many things get in the way of hearing God. Our thoughts, feelings, experiences, fears, and ambitions all create noise and distractions that can prevent us from hearing the voice of God clearly in our lives.

Every spiritual exercise is designed to help us hear the voice of God more clearly. There is absolutely no doubt in my mind that the Rosary helps us hear God's voice with greater clarity. But in order to hear the voice of God clearly, we need to allow him to bring a new order to our lives. God loves order.

We may live hectic lives in a chaotic and confusing world, but we still yearn for peace and order. There is a natural order to things, and it is in that order that we find peace. Our lives can become disordered very easily. Our ancient Catholic spirituality is constantly inviting us to establish the deep roots of order in our lives.

When I walk into Mass on Sunday, I know God is going to try to rearrange my priorities. The question is, will I let him? Every Sunday when I listen to the Gospel, I realize, "I have to change my life," or "I am still a long way from the person God wants me to be," or "There is still a lot of work for me to do." What I have realized over time is that God is constantly trying to rearrange our priorities.

When you fall in love with someone, your priorities change. Love rearranges our priorities. How much do you love? One way to measure that is by exploring how willing you are to rearrange your priorities. God wants to rearrange our priorities and put things in order. If we let him do this, we will be happier than we ever thought possible in this lifetime, and finally then we will come to know the peace that all men and women yearn for, but that so few ever really find.

But God will not force these priorities upon us. He invites us to choose them. So much of life comes down to the decisions we make. Since I spent five years of my life working on *DECISION POINT: The Dynamic Catholic Confirmation Experience,* decision making has been one of the central themes in my presentations. I am absolutely convinced that God wants us to become phenomenal decision makers. It is an essential life skill that greatly increases our chances of having a vibrant spiritual life and living an authentic life. Life is choices; we are constantly making them. Our lives are a collection of our choices and decisions.

I am equally convinced that it is almost impossible to overstate the importance of listening as a life skill and a spiritual discipline. A few weeks ago, a high school student asked me, "If you were me, what two skills would you work on improving?" I responded, "Decision making and listening." These two skills intersect with every single aspect of daily life.

The Rosary will focus you. It will calm your heart, mind, and spirit so you can hear the voice of God. It will open your heart so you can recognize him at work in your life. It will lead you to make better decisions, become a better listener, and get clear about what matters most and what matters least, and it will fill your life with peace and order.

THE ROSARY IN MY LIFE

If all of this is true, why doesn't everyone pray the Rosary a lot more? The reasons are many and simple. First off, we do have a tendency toward selfishness, and we are attracted to things that are not good for us. At times we are in love with everything that is good and right, ordered and just; at other times we crave things that create obvious disorder in our lives. We are conflicted.

In my upcoming book *Rediscover the Saints*, I write about how the saints have always been with us, around us at every time in our lives. Whether we recognized them or not, they were there. In the same way, I think the Rosary has always been with us and around us. You may have seen your grandmother praying it when you were a child, or you may have noticed that a friend's father had the beads hanging from the rearview mirror in his car. Maybe you prayed the Rosary with your family growing up, and maybe you saw it used as a necklace by a movie star or in a taxi. It was there.

I don't know if my journey with the Rosary has been more interesting or less interesting than anyone else's. My parents raised me as a Catholic, but we never prayed the Rosary together as a family. I have a very strong memory of my fourth-grade teacher giving every student in the class a rosary, and telling us a story about the powerful role it had played in her life. I don't remember the details, but I know I was moved, and thirty years later, I still have that rosary.

My fifth-grade teacher, Mr. Greck, used to pray the Rosary every day in the chapel during lunchtime. Every morning we would hear the announcement, "The Rosary will be prayed in the school chapel at 1:00 p.m. today. All are welcome." Every day he would personally invite the class to come. Nobody would go. Sometimes if you got detention, he would make you go. It was open to the whole school—twelve hundred boys, all the teachers, and the administration staff. There were usually only five or six people there. I know because I got detention a few times. Mr. Greck was a bit different. We didn't understand him at the time because he had different priorities. He wanted to prepare us to be men living for God in the world, but we wouldn't listen.

Many years later I asked him why he had prayed the Rosary every day and invited the whole school to come for years and years, and kept doing it even though nobody really came. He told me a story about his son, who had been very sick as a child. He begged God to heal him. He begged Mary to ask God to heal him. He took his son to Lourdes and begged for his healing, and his son was healed. Cured. Illness gone. Miraculous, incredible. Unbelievable stuff. He told me he was just saying thank you. The older I get, the more I think that my fifth-grade teacher, John Xavier Greck, might have been a saint.

It wasn't until I was about fifteen that I ever prayed the Rosary in earnest. Around that time I was in a youth group at our parish, and we went on a retreat and prayed the Rosary. Like most teenagers, I was restless during that time in my life. But praying the Rosary had a peaceful impact on me. I vividly remember being surprised by that at the time.

A few months later one of my best friends invited me to a prayer group. I had never heard of a prayer group. But he was a very good friend of mine, so as often happens, friendship became the bridge toward the next stage of my spiritual growth. The prayer group met every Wednesday night, praying the Rosary, reading from the Bible, and discussing the reading. I went the first time because I didn't really want to say no to my friend. I went the second time because I discovered a girl I really liked was in the prayer group. God will use whatever he has to use to get our attention.

I don't know how it happened, or even exactly when it happened, but it was around that time that I started praying the Rosary every day on my own. Looking back it is baffling to me. When I think about the average fifteen-year-old, and who I was as a teenager, I simply have no explanation for how this came about and continued. But it did.

By the time I first started traveling and speaking, in the early 1990s, I was nineteen, and I was praying three Rosaries a day—all fifteen mysteries. (The Luminous Mysteries did not come about until 2002.) In some ways it was a wonderful period in my life. All I did, really, was read, write, pray, and speak. It was a time of intense silence, solitude, and reflection.

I have been speaking and writing for twenty-five years now. Doesn't life go by in the blink of an eye? People often say to me, "I loved your first book." I ask, "What did you like about it?" It very quickly becomes clear that they are not talking about my first book. Many people think my first book was *A Call to Joy*, because it was the first to be published by a major publisher. Even more believe that my first book was *The Rhythm of Life*, because it was my first certified best seller. My first book was actually a small one, *Prayer & the Rosary*. How did a nineteen-year-old sit down and write a book about prayer? I don't know. And why? I don't know. After twenty-five years I have stopped trying to understand it all. Acceptance is more peaceful.

THE SEASONS OF LIFE

There are different seasons in our lives. There are different seasons in our spiritual journeys. Over these past three decades, the Rosary has played varying roles in my life and in my spirituality, but it has always had a place. There have been times when I have prayed it less because I felt called to explore other forms of prayer, and there have been times when I have prayed it less because I was lazy or just didn't want to. But when I have had the desire, discipline, or grace to pray the Rosary, it has always borne fruit.

When I am tempted to set the Rosary aside, I am always reminded that many of the people I would like to be more like in this world pray it. So many of the saints and the ordinary people who have nourished my spiritual life are faithfully devoted to it.

There is just something about the Rosary. It's a very powerful way to pray. In some ways I can explain it, and I have tried to the best of my ability in these pages. In other ways I cannot explain it; there is a certain mystery to it that each person has to experience for himself or herself.

It just works. When I pray the Rosary, I am a better person. It makes me a better son, brother, husband, father, employer, neighbor, citizen, and a better member of the human family. It brings an incredible peace; it teaches us to slow down, calm down, let go, surrender, and listen. The Rosary teaches us how to just be, and that is not a small or insignificant lesson. In some ways it is the perfect prayer for busy people in a busy, noisy, confused world.

② A Unique Perspective

Mary is the most famous woman in history. She has inspired more art and music than any other woman, and even in the modern age, she fascinates the imaginations of men and women of all faiths. In our own age, Mary has appeared on the cover of *Time* magazine more often than any other person.

I suspect that if we are to reconcile the great disharmony that exists between the role of men and the role of women in modern society, we will need the insight and wisdom of this great feminine role model. Is it possible for us to understand the dignity, value, mystery, and wonder of women without first understanding this woman?

At the same time, despite her fame and people's fascination with her, Mary has largely been rejected as a role model for women in the modern age. In fact, she has been rejected on an industrial scale as a model for anything. What does that say about our times? Are we confused? Do we value different things than other people in other times? Do we value the wrong things? And if so, what are we willing to do about it?

Beyond her fame and personal attributes, Mary's historical importance and significance as a feminine role model is her centrality to Christian life. The first Christians gathered around her for comfort and guidance, yet many modern

Catholics treat her as though she has some contagious disease. And of course, our non-Catholic Christian brothers and sisters generally minimize Mary's role and importance. One of the great challenges we face as modern Catholics is to find a genuine place for her in our spirituality.

When my wife gave birth to our first child, Walter, it transformed my spirituality in unexpected ways. Being a father for the first time filled me with so many new spiritual insights. Today I am blessed with five wonderful children, each unique and special in his or her own way. I love my children so much, and if I can love them so much, with all my brokenness and all my limitations, how much more God must love me? Through my children I have experienced the love of God in a whole new way.

I yearn to be with my children. When I am on the road, or even at the office for the day, I long to get home and hold them, play with them, be with them. It strikes me that perhaps above everything else, God just yearns to be with us.

The birth of my children has renewed and heightened my relationship with Mary. It has occurred to me many times that no matter how much I love my children, my wife will always have a unique perspective on their lives. It doesn't mean that she loves them more, or that I love them less. It just means that a mother sees her child's life in a way that nobody else can. If I don't take time occasionally to ask her about this motherly perspective, I unnecessarily miss a part of my children's lives.

A mother has a unique perspective. Nobody sees the life of a child the way that child's mother does—not even the father. This is Mary's perspective of Jesus' life. She has a unique perspective. It seems to me that every genuine Christian, not just Catholics, should be interested in that perspective—and not just interested, but fascinated. In the Rosary we ponder the life of Jesus through the eyes of his mother. This is an incredibly powerful experience if we enter into it fully.

DO CATHOLICS WORSHIP MARY?

It is fascinating to me that Mary, who was so instrumental in the life of Jesus, is so easily set aside and forgotten by so many Christians. Many more are clearly uncomfortable with any type of Marian spirituality. For hundreds of years this discomfort was relegated to non-Catholic Christians, but with every passing decade for about the past fifty years, more and more Catholics have become uncomfortable with Marian spirituality and comfortable ignoring Mary's role in our lives and the life of the Church.

This is in large part the result of the relentless questioning of Mary's place in Christian spirituality by non-Catholic Christians. The question they have been posing over and over for five hundred years is: Why do Catholics worship Mary?

Why haven't we answered this question once and for all for the whole world? It's astounding when you step back and think about the damage this one question has done to the faith of millions of Catholics and to the Church as a whole. The answer is that we have become hypnotized by complexity. The Catholic faith is so rich and deep and broad that the average Catholic struggles to know what matters most or even where to start. People need simple starting points.

Why do Catholics worship Mary? Even the way the question is formulated assumes that what they are questioning is an accepted fact. It is not a question seeking truth or understanding; it is a question that seeks to trap. The question starts out with the assumption that Catholics worship Mary. It doesn't start out with truth-seeking curiosity, asking, *"Do Catholics worship Mary?"*

Anytime you are being attacked with questions, the first rule is always: Don't accept the premise of the question.

This constant questioning for five hundred years, which began with the Protestant Reformation and has been carried on by modern evangelical Christianity, has played a role in slowly but surely eroding the faith of Catholics.

We are now at the point where most modern Catholics don't have a dynamic relationship with Mary, are generally uncomfortable or suspicious of the role she plays in Catholic liturgy and spirituality, and look down on the Rosary as something from another place and time that has no relevance in their complex modern lives.

For hundreds of years, our non-Catholic Christian brothers and sisters have been accusing us of worshipping Mary (and the saints), and I don't think we have done a good job of settling this question. It is fascinating, disturbing, and tragic that we have failed to articulate and widely circulate a short, compelling answer to the question. This single failure has altered the history of modern Catholicism, by sowing faith-eroding doubts. We should have equipped every Catholic on the planet with an answer to the question: Do Catholics worship Mary?

No. We pray to Mary, but not in the same way we pray to God—and not to worship her as a deity.

Think of it in this way: If you got sick and asked me to pray for you, I would. This does not make me uniquely Catholic, or even uniquely Christian. There are many non-Christians who believe in the power of prayer. If I ask my non-Catholic Christian friends whether they pray for their spouses or their children, they will all say yes. If I ask them to pray for me, they will say yes.

Our relationship with Mary operates under this same principle. We believe that Mary and the saints are dead to this world, but we also believe they live on with God for eternity in the next world. And we believe that their prayers are just as powerful now that they are in heaven—even more powerful— than they were when they were here on earth. We are essentially saying to them, "We have problems down here. You know what it is like, because you have been here. Please, pray for us!"

Our non-Catholic Christian friends don't believe people can still pray in the afterlife. We do. Our spiritual universe is bigger than theirs. In fact, one of the most incredible things about our Catholic faith is the vastness of our spiritual universe.

We could, of course, dive much deeper into the question, but the average Catholic needs an answer he or she can remember and articulate when questioned. We need this answer to protect our own faith from doubts creeping in, but we also need it so we can defend our faith against errors, have confidence in our Catholicism, and speak boldly about this common objection.

Devotion to Mary is a legitimate part of Christian spirituality. It is also an authentic path to God and heroic virtue.

•••••••

This one objection—that Catholics worship Mary— always gets me wondering how we ever let it get this far. Our non-Catholic Christian brothers and sisters have five very specific objections to Catholicism:

1. The pope is just another man.
2. Catholics are idolaters who worship Mary and the saints.
3. Scripture itself is the sole authority; the Catholic Church does not have the exclusive authority to interpret the Scriptures.
4. The Eucharist is only a symbol.
5. We are saved by faith alone, not by faith and good works.

They have many other criticisms of Catholics and Catholicism—and these are two categories, separate but connected—but most of their other objections and criticisms are connected to the preceding five.

For five hundred years we have been letting them bombard us with these questions that make the average Catholic want to hide under the table. This leads many good-hearted Catholics to have an intense moment of embarrassment. Being embarrassed about your faith is not a good thing. The negative psychological impact of this is massive, and sooner or later it will lead to negative spiritual effects also.

What makes me sad is that this could be so easily avoided. Why have we not schooled every Catholic to answer these five questions? Imagine if we developed clear, concise, and compelling answers to these five main objections; gave a copy to every Catholic; and explained these issues to them in five homilies, one objection each week, once a year—it would be an amazing thing. Picture every parish in the country doing this for the same five weeks each year. It is good and noble to do unique things in every parish, but some things we need to do on an industrial scale, for every Catholic and every parish. We need to start thinking on a completely different level. Giving Catholics confidence to talk about their faith and answer objections is essential to the success of the New Evangelization and the future of Catholicism.

We need a small book that answers those five objections in language that is accessible and inspiring, logical and compelling. It's time. I will write that book soon.

Love and devotion to Mary is a part of Christianity that can be traced back to the very first Christians. Who is Mary to you? What role does she play in your spiritual life? Are you struggling to get focused spiritually or looking for a way to grow to new heights? These are all questions we should ponder from time to time.

There are many ways to focus our relationship with God. Many holy men and women of monumental virtue considered Mary's humility to be a sure path to intimacy with God. They have surrendered themselves completely to Mary's protection and guidance, begging her to lead them ever closer to her son.

Who are your heroes? If the mother of one of your heroes invited you to lunch, how excited would you be? What would you talk about? Would you give her a message to pass along to her son? Too often we squeeze the humanity out of our spiritual perspectives and exercises. Mary was a woman, a wife, a mother, a human—and the mother of Jesus. She laughed and cried, made dinner, changed diapers, and suffered anguish we will never know. If Mary invited you to lunch, what would you ask her?

I wish I had her courage. I'd ask her what she knew about Jesus and his future, and when she knew it. Then I'd ask her how she had the courage to face each day knowing what she knew was going to unfold.

It's all about Jesus, but just as we learn much about the life, teachings, and person of Jesus from the Gospels, we can learn much about him from Mary. She has a unique perspective. She can teach us things about Jesus that nobody else can.

③

Praying with Beads

Catholics were not the first to pray with beads. The exact origin of prayer beads is unknown. Men and women of many faiths have used beads to pray. The word *bead* in English is derived from an Old English word that means "prayer," and the earliest image of a string of beads is found in a fresco in Santorini, Greece, dating back to the seventeenth century BC. The earliest widespread use of prayer beads appears to have been in the eighth century BC, among Hindus.

The Greeks use *komboloi*, which are commonly called worry beads. They have an odd number of beads on a strand, typically seventeen or twenty-one. While referred to as worry beads, they seem to be used for all kinds of reasons, but none of them religious. The Greeks use these beads for relaxation, to guard against bad luck, as a symbol of social prestige, to reduce the urge to smoke, or simply to pass the time.

Buddhists and Hindus use *japa mala*, which is made up of 108 beads, twenty-seven that are repeated four times. Eastern Orthodox Christians use a knotted rosary made up of one hundred knots. Islamic prayer beads usually have ninety-nine or thirty-three beads. Roman Catholics use a rosary made up of fifty-nine beads. (The word *rosary* is derived from the Latin word *rosarium*, which means "rose garden.")

So praying with beads certainly wasn't an original idea, but it serves powerfully to remind us that everything before the coming of Jesus was preparing for that moment, and that God yearns to transform everything into something holy, even something as ordinary as a small rope with some beads on it.

The purpose of prayer beads is almost universally to allow the person to keep track of the number of prayers that have been said, while at the same time focusing on the deeper meaning of the prayers themselves.

ORIGINS OF THE ROSARY

The history of the Rosary is interwoven with the history of the Church, the early development of Christian prayer in general, and the evolution of the Hail Mary itself, which is obviously central to the Rosary. It has been evolving since the earliest Christian times; in fact, it could be argued that the roots of the Rosary lead back to before the coming of Christ.

The Desert Fathers were Christian hermits and monks living in the Egyptian desert beginning in the third century AD. They used stones or pebbles to keep track of their prayers. The pebbles were collected in a bowl, and they removed one stone as they prayed each of the 150 psalms.

It is believed that the first Christian prayer ropes were developed in the late third or early fourth century by St. Anthony, one of the Desert Fathers. As Christian religious communities sprang up in different parts of the world, whole religious orders began praying the psalms using these first Christian prayer ropes. These had fifty knots on them and would be prayed three times to account for each of the 150 psalms.

It was also around this time that some form of the Jesus Prayer began to emerge, and the beads were used to repeat it. The Jesus Prayer is a short prayer that has also changed over the centuries, said repeatedly in a type of mantra while counting beads. (A mantra is a word or phrase repeated frequently.) This prayer has always been significantly more popular among Eastern Catholics than among Roman Catholics. Though it has experienced resurgence among Western Catholics over the past thirty years, its popularity can't match the massive popularity of the Rosary, even as practice of the Rosary has been declining over that same period.

The earliest form of the Jesus Prayer appears to have been: "Lord Jesus Christ, Son of God, have mercy on me" or "Lord Jesus Christ, Son of God, have mercy on us." The most common form used today is: "Lord Jesus Christ, Son of God, have mercy on me, a sinner."

It is unclear when the phrase "a sinner" was added to the formula. But even today there are many different versions of the Jesus Prayer, the simplest being just the name Jesus, which is repeated continuously on each bead.

For monks who could not read the psalms, the Jesus Prayer became a powerful form of personal prayer. But its use was not confined to those who could not read. The wisdom of the Desert Fathers celebrated simplicity as a path to God, and this method of prayer was almost universally adopted by the monks of that era between the third and fifth centuries.

The *Catechism of the Catholic Church* is made up of four parts; the last is dedicated Christian prayer. Here we find the Jesus Prayer discussed from paragraphs 2665 to 2669. Let's briefly take a look at paragraphs 2666 and 2667.

2666 The one name that contains everything is the one that the Son of God received in his incarnation: JESUS. The divine name may not be spoken by human lips, but by assuming our humanity the Word of God hands it over to us and we can invoke it: "Jesus," "YHWH saves." The name "Jesus" contains all: God and man and the whole economy of creation and salvation. To pray "Jesus" is to invoke him and to call him within us. His name is the only one that contains the presence it signifies. Jesus is the Risen One, and whoever invokes the name of Jesus is welcoming the Son of God who loved him and who gave himself up for him.

2667 This simple invocation of faith developed in the tradition of prayer under many forms in East and West. The most usual formulation, transmitted by the spiritual writers of the Sinai, Syria, and Mt. Athos, is the invocation, "Lord Jesus Christ, Son of God, have mercy on us sinners." It combines the Christological hymn of Philippians 2:6–11 with the cry of the publican and the blind men begging for light.

I was introduced to the Jesus Prayer in my late twenties by a Byzantine priest, and I have used it at different times and in different seasons of my spiritual life ever since. There have been times in my own life when I have been so tired, disoriented, and overwhelmed that this was the only prayer I could pray.

NOT A SINGLE EVENT

The development of the Rosary was slow, and it had many turns along the way. Not only was it evolving over the centuries, but it was also inspiring other spiritual practices with the same beads—and with different beads.

Before long Pope Gregory the Great (590–604) instituted praying the Hail Mary during the Mass on the Fourth Sunday of Advent. It was at this point that its popularity began to spread.

The earliest version of the prayer consisted only of the angel Gabriel's words, with Mary's name inserted: "Hail Mary, full of grace, the Lord is with thee." The words of Elizabeth ("Blessed art thou among women and blessed is the fruit of thy womb") weren't added until much later, around AD 1050. After that, we begin to find many examples of individuals praying the Hail Mary in a repetitive fashion, using a string of beads to count their prayers.

Genuflection (making the Sign of the Cross with your right knee to the ground) and prostration (lying flat on your chest) were also often incorporated into the early practice of the Rosary. This gave it a penitential character. For example, St. Albert (1060–1140) was born in Spain and was known to recite 150 Hail Marys every day, one hundred of them accompanied by a genuflection, and prostrating himself each time for the remaining fifty.

In 1214 St. Dominic, the founder of the Dominican Order, had a vision of Mary, who presented him with the Rosary, both the beads and the prayers to be prayed. While it is still widely believed by some Dominicans and many Catholics, scholars today disagree on and debate the authenticity of this vision. What is certain is that Dominic had a tremendous devotion to Mary and the Rosary, which he promoted wherever he traveled to preach. He encouraged lay Catholics to gather in small groups to pray an early form of the Rosary together. These were quite possibly the first expressions of the prayer groups and small group communities that still have a powerful impact on people's lives today.

While the Hail Mary and the Rosary were developing, another practice had been common since the time of the early Church. This practice was to pray the Our Father 150 times. In fact, before the string of beads with five decades was called a rosary, it was referred to as a *paternoster* (Latin for "our Father"), and the craftsmen who made the beads were called *paternosterers*.

The Hail Mary was still developing, and in 1261 Pope Urban IV added the name of Jesus to the end of Elizabeth's words. But at this point the prayer did not have the final petition: "Holy Mary, Mother of God, pray for us sinners, now and at the hour of our death."

In the first half of the fourteenth century, Catholics began adding their own private petitions to the end of each Hail Mary. There is evidence of a great variety of petitions. The most common petitions asked Mary for prayers and protection.

In the fifteenth century, both the Hail Mary and the Rosary began to take the shape that we find today. Dominic of Prussia added the mysteries sometime between 1410 and 1439, and then each decade had a unique quality. By centering each decade on an event from the lives of Jesus and Mary, the prayer unleashed the spiritual imagination to contemplate these epic moments.

Dominic of Prussia also added a sentence from Scripture after each Hail Mary, further igniting the spiritual imagination; this is widely believed to be the first time the laity were encouraged to meditate while praying the Rosary. These Scripture verses are not part of the most common modern version of the Rosary; the Scriptural Rosary is still practiced by just a fraction of those who pray the Rosary regularly. I have put together a version of a Scriptural Rosary and included it later in this book for those interested in exploring that form.

A theologian who was considered an expert in the many forms of prayer was the next to influence the development and popularity of the Rosary. His name was Alan de Rupe of Brittany (1428–1475), in what is today northwest France.

The Rosary captured Alan de Rupe's imagination as a powerful tool for spiritual growth. He further understood that this prayer was for everyone. You didn't need to be a priest or a nun, a king or a queen, rich, titled, educated, or anything else. The Rosary was a democratic prayer, and it was portable, which meant that not only was it available to all people, but it was available to all people in all places at all times.

Rupe set out to massively increase the popularity of the Rosary throughout Europe, and he succeeded. He established Rosary confraternities, where members would pledge to pray fifteen decades of the Rosary each week, and to pray for each other as members of the confraternity.

The next great step for the Hail Mary came eighty years later, in 1555, when St. Peter Canisius published the Hail Mary in his catechism with almost the entire final petition. His version read at the end: "Holy Mary, Mother of God, pray for us sinners." Eleven years later, the *Catechism of the Council of Trent* (a work that Canisius was instrumental in creating) included, for the first time, the entire petition, concluding with the words "now and at the hour of our death. Amen."

The version of the Hail Mary we pray today was finally given official approval in 1568, with the publication of the new Roman Breviary. The next year Pope Pius V commended it as a devotion for all the faithful in the papal bull *Consueverunt Romani Pontifices*.

We've been using the term *Rosary* throughout our discussion, but the first recorded use of that word did not appear until 1597. For 320 years, from 1597 until 1917, the form of both the Hail Mary and the Rosary remained the same. That is an amazingly long period of stability for something that had been constantly evolving for sixteen hundred years.

During these 320 years there was much written and spoken about the Rosary. Most notable was Pope Paul VI's insight that the Rosary was a compendium of the Gospel: meaning a concise collection of writings or insights systematically ordered to maximize the experience for those who took the time and made the effort. Pope Paul VI was saying that when we pray the Rosary, we have an intense and focused summary experience of the Gospel.

FATIMA AND POPE JOHN PAUL II

Two important events, one at the beginning of the twentieth century and the other at the beginning of the twenty-first century, changed the form and experience of the Rosary forever. First, on May 13, 1917, Mary appeared to three shepherd children in Fatima, Portugal, while they were playing out in the fields. The children's names were Jacinta, Francisco, and Lucia. Mary told them to come back to that exact place on the thirteenth day of each month for the next five months, promising she would appear to them each time and entrust a message to them.

Mary also told the children of Fatima to pray for world peace by reciting the Rosary every day. This was fifty years before the idea of world peace became popular with celebrities and college students, and toward the beginning of a century of war.

On July 13, 1917, Mary asked the children to add a short prayer to the end of each decade: "O my Jesus, forgive us our sins, save us from the fires of hell, and bring all souls to heaven, especially those most in need of your mercy." Today this is referred to as the Fatima prayer, and many Catholics incorporate it into the Rosary.

The children of Fatima were clearly afraid of hell, but uniquely, not only for themselves. They were afraid for anyone who might experience hell in the afterlife, even and perhaps especially people they didn't even know. Seventy-five years later Pope John Paul II would speak about increasing the geography of our prayer. He urged Catholics to get beyond just praying for themselves, their family, their parish, and their own country. He invited Catholics to extend the geography of their prayer to touch every corner of the earth.

Seventy-five years earlier, here were these three shepherd children: Lucia was nine years old, Francisco was eight, and Jacinta was just six years old. But the geography of their prayer was global.

Pope Francis visited Fatima on May 13, 2017, to celebrate the one hundredth anniversary of the first apparition and to canonize Jacinta and Francisco.

The second event to change the form of the Rosary happened when Pope John Paul II, after the whole world had been mesmerized watching him pray the Rosary as pope for twenty-three years, made his own contribution to its evolution. On October 16, 2002, he published *Rosarium Virginis Mariae* ("Rosary of the Virgin Mary"), an apostolic letter dedicated to the Rosary. In this text he proposed that five new mysteries be added to the Rosary. He called these the Luminous Mysteries, or Mysteries of Light.

Adding the Luminous Mysteries almost six hundred years after the Joyful, Sorrowful, and Glorious Mysteries had been established was a bold move by a man who was widely known to be one of deep prayer and endless devotion to the Rosary. I wonder how many times he prayed the Luminous Mysteries before he wrote *Rosarium Virginis Mariae*. I wonder what other events in Jesus' life he considered but did not ultimately include.

The Luminous Mysteries are:

- The Baptism of Jesus in the River Jordan
- The Wedding Feast at Cana
- The Proclamation of the Kingdom of God
- The Transfiguration of Jesus
- The Institution of the Eucharist

Everything Jesus did and said revealed something about him. Those whose awareness was earthbound and caught up in the things of this world picked up on very little of what Jesus was revealing to them. Others with spiritual awareness, who were paying attention not just with their eyes and ears but with their hearts and souls, absorbed a lot more of what Jesus was revealing to them. Some days when I pray the Rosary, I belong in the former group, and some days I belong in the latter group. But these new mysteries gave us all a chance to ponder what Jesus was trying to reveal to us in new ways.

These Luminous Mysteries, these moments of light, were epic moments in the life of Jesus when his divinity exploded into ordinary human activities, revealing his astounding power—the astounding power that was so often misunderstood; the same astounding power that would ultimately lead to his execution like a common criminal.

These mysteries of light scream: "This is the chosen one, the one you have been waiting upon for so very long. This is the Messiah; this is the Son of God!" Some realized that these great powers were not displayed to gain attention or to fulfill some unmet ego need. These great powers were actually a dim reflection of his divinity. He was completely capable of putting on a fireworks display that would have gotten everyone's attention. But God is a perfect gentleman and always defends the possibility of love by respecting our free will. Most people got temporarily fascinated with Jesus' miracles, but never looked beyond them to see what they represented.

THE ROSARY TODAY

Modern Catholics in the West have all but abandoned the Rosary. If you ask them why, I'm not sure they could tell you. It has happened gradually—younger generations haven't embraced it, and older generations have left this world.

I suspect one of the reasons the Rosary has become so unpopular during this modern era is because it is stereotypically considered the prayer of an overly pious old woman with little education and too much time on her hands. In a complex world where we bow to knowledge and academic degrees, piety is considered to border on superstition, and things that are simple are often arrogantly dismissed as beneath us. We are a sophisticated, educated people now, and we have no need for those simple spiritual exercises of the past.

This declining practice of the Rosary also corresponds with the declining interest in God, religion, and spirituality in general. Hypnotized by complexity, too many people today have lost their way. They are uncertain about who they are, why they are here, what matters most, and what matters least. But they keep walking deeper and deeper into the woods, looking for answers that can only be found in the clearing.

Piety is simply a matter of having reverence for God. I've spent time around enough famous friends to see that most people have more reverence for their favorite musician or actor than they do for God. Beyond this absurdity we find that an alarming number of people have more reverence for themselves than for God.

Did you reverence God today? How? Why?

When we start thinking clearly again, we will yearn for simplicity in most things and find a hundred reasons to reverence God every day.

Catholics have abandoned the Rosary today because we have been seduced by complexity. We give our allegiance and respect to complexity, but simplicity is the key to perfection. Peace in our hearts is born from simplicity in our lives. All the great leaders throughout history have agreed that the simplest solution is usually the best solution. The genius of God is simplicity. If you wish to tap into the wonder, the glory, and the power of God, apply simplicity to your life—and start with your prayer. Pray simply.

Our lives are suffering under the intolerable weight of ever-increasing complexity. We complicate everything. And as this diseased fascination with complexity has swept across modern culture, it has also affected the way we approach prayer. Subsequently, as modern Catholics, we have deemed the Rosary as something beneath us at best and as worthless in many cases. Don't despise simplicity. There is real power in it.

Simplicity is one of the practical fruits of the Rosary. By reflecting on the moments of Jesus' and Mary's lives, we discover what matters most and what matters least, and a beautiful clarity emerges. Embrace the Rosary, and Mary will teach you how to order your heart, mind, and soul with the genius of simplicity.

The Rosary is not just a prayer for gray-haired old ladies with too much time on their hands. It is a rich practice of prayer we can all benefit from. This is the dissenting opinion, the truth ignored. We probably need the Rosary more today than at any other time in history, but we are less able to embrace it than at any other time in history because of our misplaced values, our warped worldview, and our brash exaggerated confidence in our own intellect.

The Rosary is ancient, yet ever new and always fresh. It is a spiritual practice for the men and women of any era and all ages. For all those who engage it, it rewards them a hundred times for their efforts. It is that ancient treasure map that has led countless men and women from all walks of life to the riches of peace, joy, clarity, and contentment. But don't take my word for it. Try it for yourself.

THE ROSARY IS EVER ANCIENT AND EVER NEW

For more than two thousand years, the Rosary has been evolving and changing. The Hail Mary prayer came together slowly; it took more than a thousand years. We have added things to the practice and taken things from it. I don't know anyone who genuflects one hundred times or prostrates himself fifty times like St. Albert did.

Has the Rosary become the-best-version-of-itself? Only God knows. But if it hasn't, we will see more changes in the future. Then again, perhaps in every age the Rosary has been the-best-version-of-itself for the people of those times. Maybe it evolves to meet us where we are in our spiritual journey as a Church, to meet some need we have, possibly one that we are not even aware of.

The point is that some things are a mystery. It's good to have a little mystery in your life. If everything could be known, understood, explained, and clearly proven, there would be no room for faith—which appears to be essential to God's plan for the world and humanity.

So, with all that we know about the past, we are invited to step bravely into an uncertain future. It is our spirituality that gives us the courage to step boldly into this uncertain future, hoping for good things. Now we have stumbled upon one of the greatest spiritual traits: the ability to enjoy uncertainty. Not *tolerate* it, but *enjoy* it. The Rosary has been helping ordinary and extraordinary people to enjoy uncertainty for hundreds of years. Learning to enjoy uncertainty, surrendering to God's abundant providence, is an extraordinary spiritual gift from God—and it's just one of the many gifts he wants to give you through the Rosary.

(4)

Dynamic Prayer

Prayer by its very nature is dynamic. What comes to mind when you hear the word *dynamic*? By definition it means "ever fresh, ever new, constantly growing or progressing; a force that stimulates change or progress with a system or process."

Prayer is dynamic. It is ever fresh, always new. A daily habit of prayer is like the tide—the waves just keep coming in and out, and over time they change the coastline. Prayer drives progress. It is a force that stimulates change. It is a powerful process that is constantly evolving to continually transform you into the-very-best-version-of-yourself. We ignore it at times and neglect it at others, forgetting that prayer is an unimaginable gift from God.

MEETING PEOPLE WHERE THEY ARE

When Dynamic Catholic was founded, we adopted the phrase "meeting people where they are" as one of our central principles. Too often, most ministry stops a few miles short of where people really are. Like a president who doesn't know how much a gallon of milk costs, when we are trying to lead others closer to God, we are often out of touch with where people *really* are.

Meeting people where they are is easy to say and incredibly difficult to do.

Dynamic prayer meets people where they are and leads them one step closer to God with each encounter. The Rosary is a powerful form of dynamic prayer. It is ever fresh, ever new, and, like a faithful friend, is patient with us, encourages us to grow, challenges us to change, and comforts us in times of doubt, discouragement, and confusion. It is also arranged around a process that constantly transforms us into more of who God created us to be. At the same time, because of the way it invites us to reflect on how the prayers and mysteries relate to our own lives, it is deeply personal.

How does the Rosary accomplish all this? It doesn't change every time we pray it. It was the same last year as it is today, yet we can have a completely different experience of it today than we did yesterday or last week. It doesn't change, but we do. Our questions change. Our struggles and concerns change. Our faith and doubts change. Where we are in our journey with God changes. The Rosary provides the context, the format, and the process for God to speak to us about all these things.

It is quite astounding if you really take time to reflect on it. Unfortunately in our unthinking, shallow culture, the Rosary is seen as ancient, static, and irrelevant. And these days there are fewer witnesses who are willing to stand up and say: The Rosary will heal your history, bring peace to your soul, help you develop dynamic relationships, help you with your unresolved fears, transform your life, heal your soul, and so much more.

Who doesn't need their history healed? Who doesn't want dynamic relationships? Who doesn't want to be rescued from the turbulence and anxiety of modern life and given a steady heart to ride the waves of this life?

Every time you pray the Rosary, Jesus welcomes you into his life and you welcome him into yours. Only great things can happen when you invite Jesus into your life.

The Rosary is truly a dynamic prayer.

• • • • • • •

One thing that became abundantly clear during Dynamic Catholic's research project that explored the difference between highly engaged and disengaged Catholics was the indisputable importance of daily prayer. What I before suspected, I now knew for sure: A daily routine of prayer is the primary driver of engagement among Christians. The realization came crashing down upon me that if I spent the rest of my life just helping people to develop a daily routine of prayer, it would be a life very well spent.

I spent many months pondering the best way to go about this, and during that time, this question emerged: If you could get every Catholic to pray in the same way for ten minutes each day, how would you encourage them to spend that ten minutes?

Now, you may be expecting me to mention the Rosary, but no, because the Rosary takes more than ten minutes. Of course, there are more reasons than that, but they are not relevant here.

What was needed was a form of prayer that would be highly engaging to both the beginner and the person who is quite advanced in the spiritual life. It had to be a form of prayer that could be taught very quickly and easily, ideally one that could be contained on something the size of a business card.

This is how The Prayer Process came about. It has taught millions of people to pray, and given real form to a daily prayer experience. But its real power is found in the way it expands or contracts according to what a person is dealing with in his or her life at that very moment. It meets people where they are.

Just as a symphony is built around four very distinct movements, The Prayer Process is built around seven very distinct aspects of prayer that intersect with daily life and the universal struggle to be fully who God created us to be as human beings. Let's take a quick look at the seven parts of the process.

THE PRAYER PROCESS

1. **Gratitude:** Begin by thanking God in a personal dialogue for whatever you are most grateful for today.
2. **Awareness:** Revisit the times in the past twenty-four hours when you were and were not the-best-version-of-yourself. Talk to God about these situations and what you learned from them.
3. **Significant Moments:** Identify something you experienced today and explore what God might be trying to say to you through that event (or person).
4. **Peace:** Ask God to forgive you for any wrong you have committed (against yourself, another person, or him) and to fill you with a deep and abiding peace.
5. **Freedom:** Speak with God about how he is inviting you to change your life, so that you can experience the freedom to be the-best-version-of-yourself.
6. **Others:** Lift up to God anyone you feel called to pray for today, asking him to bless and guide them.
7. Finish by praying the **Our Father**.

Each of the seven movements in The Prayer Process deals with an enormous spiritual theme, but on the level of what is happening in each person's life. Rather than saying, "That is sinful and you really shouldn't be doing it—you must stop that now," The Prayer Process approaches our sinfulness from the angle of freedom—which is a massive spiritual topic and the yearning of every human heart—and asks us to speak with God about how he is inviting us to change our lives.

The Prayer Process has the ability to expand or contract according to where a person is in his or her spiritual journey. A seventy-five-year-old Carthusian monk with ten thousand hours of prayer experience could pray The Prayer Process and have a dynamic experience. At the same time, someone who is just trying to establish the habit of prayer in his or her life could pray The Prayer Process and have just as dynamic an experience as the monk. They both use the same format or prayer, but they pray about very different things—yet they both have powerful and dynamic experiences.

In the same way, each set of mysteries of the Rosary is made up of five movements that lead us to ponder very specific events in the lives of Jesus and Mary, and the lessons they hold for our own lives today. The Carthusian monk and the beginner could pray the Joyful Mysteries and, again, both have powerful, dynamic experiences even though their meditations would be vastly different.

God wants to meet us in prayer, and he is happy to meet us where we are. Any other way leads us to pretend we are someone we are not, and if there is one place we should be completely who we are, devoid of all pretense and guile, it is in prayer. Pretending to be someone we are not in prayer is a tragic, self-defeating lie.

The Rosary is ever new, not because it changes, but because we change. The stream of life carries us constantly to new places, and the Rosary meets us there to help us make sense of those new places and the challenges and opportunities that come with them.

PRAYER MIRRORS LOVE

Dynamic forms of prayer mirror both love and intimacy. Love is creative. The lover looks for new and special ways to spend time with the beloved, but also cherishes the ordinary and regular ways they spend time together. Lovers do not go to the same restaurant at the same time every week and have the same conversation. They may go to the same restaurant, on the same day, at the same time, but they would not have the same conversation. Why? Different things have happened in their lives and inside them, and their relationship faces new opportunities and new difficulties. Love is dynamic.

Prayer also mirrors intimacy. Intimacy is mutual self-revelation. By speaking with God about our deepest hopes and dreams, fears and failures, we form an incredible intimacy with him. This is not a human initiative. God reaches out to us first. Everything in life is a response to his invitation. He desires intimacy, so from the very beginning, in everything he has said and done, he has been revealing himself to us. Intimacy is dynamic.

Love, intimacy, and prayer are all deeply personal. Each of these inspires and provokes us in a variety of ways that ultimately should lead us to love more and want with all our hearts to be better people. This manifests in our daily lives in many different ways, but let's consider just one. If you ask someone

40

who is deeply in love, "When do you think about her?" he will say, "All the time." It's not true. He hasn't purposely lied, but he is deceived. The truth is, he thinks about her in the gaps. When he is absorbed in his work or any other activity, he is focused on and thinking about what he is doing—and not thinking about his beloved. But when he takes a break or gets distracted for a moment, his mind goes first to his beloved. Every gap in his day is filled with this person he loves, and he hopes he can fill every gap in her life also.

Love fills the gaps. Our conversation with God should be constant throughout the day. As we mature spiritually we find ourselves talking to God about matters at work and at home, and talking to him in the gaps of our day. Even if we spend those gaps thinking about our beloved, we talk to God about her and our love for her.

One of the curses that smartphones have brought upon the world is that they rob us of these gaps. Most people reach for their smartphones as soon as anything that vaguely resembles a gap in their lives emerges. At the stoplight, in line at the supermarket, in restaurants—people are obsessed with their devices. Walking down the street, in the waiting room at the doctor's office—almost everywhere we go people are attached to their phones.

We have become people of the device. It robs us of countless opportunities throughout the day to turn to God for a brief, informal conversation. It kills intimacy and connection. It robs us of our ability to give each other our undivided attention. The device kills deep listening. It prevents us from looking deeply into someone's eyes and really listening to what he or she is saying. We are called to become people of prayer, not people of the device.

Prayer invites us into an ever-deeper intimacy with God, and in that intimacy, he teaches us how to be intimate with each other. Prayer is looking deeply into God's eyes and giving him our undivided attention.

SO MANY WAYS

There is more to praying the Rosary than just saying the prayers. Anyone can say the Rosary—just teach them the words and they can rattle them off. But authentic prayer requires mindfulness and intentionality: the mindfulness to be present and set aside all the distractions of our lives as best we can, and the intentionality to align our will with God's—for clarity around a decision we need to make, for a favor from him, for forgiveness, for freedom in an area of our lives where we feel enslaved, or any of the infinite number of intentions we can bring to any experience of prayer. The point is, the Rosary is not magic. There is no deal making with God. So many Rosaries mindlessly rattled off don't equal a prayer answered by God.

Prayer doesn't change God; prayer changes us. It's not about convincing him of our will; it's about surrendering to his will. It is more rewarding to approach prayer seeking to understand God, rather than in search of some favor. If we approach prayer in hopes of growing in virtue and genuinely seeking his will, we will never be disappointed.

There are many ways to pray the Rosary; the same prayer can be approached in different ways. The first and most obvious is to focus on the words, which are deeply rooted in the Scriptures and Christian tradition. The Our Father was, of course, given to us by Jesus himself (see Matthew 6:9–13). The Creed represents the first expression of Christian conviction. The first part of the Hail Mary comes from the message delivered by the angel to Mary in Nazareth: "Hail, full of grace. The Lord is with you" (Luke 1:28). This greeting is then followed by the words Elizabeth used to greet Mary during the Visitation: "Blessed are you among women, and blessed is the fruit of your womb" (Luke 1:42). The Glory Be is the simplest expression of Christian praise and belief in the triune God. And from the times of antiquity, Christians have placed themselves under the name of God and the sign of redemption, thus giving us the Sign of the Cross.

You may choose to focus on the words sometimes. If I may make a suggestion, focus on a word or phrase. Every word and every phrase is so rich with meaning, you will find yourself constantly distracted. Focusing on a single word or phrase will limit these distractions. It's unlikely it will eliminate the distractions altogether, but it will allow you to get to a deeper place.

For example, you may choose to focus on the phrase *full of grace* today. Tomorrow you may find yourself especially in need of forgiveness, so you may choose to focus on *pray for us sinners*. On another day you may focus simply on the single word *with* from the phrase *the Lord is with you*, and ponder what it means to be *with* the Lord. It's amazing how deeply we can meditate just on the word *with*. What does it mean to be with the Lord?

The words of the Rosary are powerful and filled with layers of meaning, but so are the mysteries that we use as a backdrop to each decade. There may be times in your life when you are so distracted and overwhelmed that you don't need another word in your day. On those occasions you may choose to meditate on the mysteries. Just allow the words to float by subconsciously. Get lost in the scene. Imagine yourself there, at Jesus' side. Place yourself in the scene, not as a fly on the wall, but as a very specific person, so you can fully immerse yourself in the situation and explore what you would have been thinking and feeling if you were there.

In part two the reflections will focus on this approach of placing yourself in the scene. But whether you choose to focus on the words, to meditate on the mysteries, or some other approach, one thing is certain: Your mind cannot do two things at once. This is where many people become discouraged with praying the Rosary. They try to pray the words and meditate on the mystery at the same time. Impossible! We must decide between the two. Your mind was created to focus on one thing at a time. Ultimately it was created to focus on God. When we try to focus on more than one thing at the same time, our mind goes back and forth between the two, often at an alarming rate. While this may give the appearance of thinking about both things at once, it is a deception. The mind can only focus on one thing at a time. Trying to focus on more than one thing at a time most likely will make the Rosary an exhausting exercise.

When you do choose to focus on the words, it may help to meditate on the mystery for a few moments before each decade. At the same time, it is critical to remember that the Rosary is not a mental exercise alone. The disposition of your heart is what matters most. Place your heart in the loving presence of Mary. Allow her to comfort you, to love you. Your mind will follow your heart. It is possible to be too much like Martha when praying the Rosary (see Luke 10:38–42). It is easy to fall into the trap of trying so hard to do it all right and then miss out on the peace that Jesus and Mary want to flood our hearts with during the Rosary.

I also find it very fruitful to offer each decade for a person or a special intention. There are so many people and situations that I want to pray for, and so many people who ask me to pray for them. Offering each decade for a person or a situation helps me to stay focused.

Another way to pray the Rosary is with the Scriptures. In chapter 10 I have included an example of a Scriptural Rosary, which simply involves reading or reflecting upon one line of Scripture before each Hail Mary.

The other thing to be aware of as you approach an extended spiritual exercise such as the Rosary is that distractions are inevitable. If you started to pray the Rosary and went back to the beginning and began again every time you got distracted, you would never finish praying.

Distractions are an inevitable and unavoidable part of prayer. There are things you can do to minimize them, but you cannot eliminate them. Some days you will have fewer than others—resist the temptation to equate that with good prayer. There will be other days when it seems that all you do the whole time is get distracted. Don't equate that with bad prayer.

Are distractions good or bad? Neither. Like so many things, they are neutral until we touch them. How you respond to a distraction is good or bad, but not the distraction itself. First, you cannot do anything about the distraction until you realize you are distracted. Once you realize it, that is your moment. What will you do? Get lost in the distraction or return to your prayer?

Which is better for you, ten push-ups or one hundred? One hundred. Why? Every push-up strengthens your muscles. Every distraction is an opportunity to strengthen your spiritual muscles. You realize you are distracted, you return to your prayer, and in that moment what happens? You choose God over the distraction, you pull your mind and likely your heart away from the distraction, and you align your heart and mind with God. That's a spiritual push-up.

I could go on for another hundred pages just with these little thoughts, but we learn to pray best by praying. But to offer one last, very practical insight, let me just say: Don't race. There is a tendency to race through the prayers of the Rosary. Take your time. Rushing will rob you of the fruits, especially the peace I have spoken of so often. It's not a race. I'd rather that you prayed three decades slowly and thoughtfully than fifteen decades at warp speed.

People frequently ask me how often they should pray the Rosary, or how often I pray it. These are perhaps the wrong questions. I prefer the question: How do I become so enchanted with the Rosary that I yearn to pray it constantly and have to drag myself away from it? But we are human, and we are constantly asking God and others to set a limit on how much we have to love, give, do, be. We love rules for all the wrong reasons. In the context of rules, we devise ways to do what we want to do and still fulfill God's requirements. This kind of thinking is born out of a deep-seated mentality of minimalism: What is the least I can do? But the lover doesn't ask this question. This question is offensive to the lover. And it certainly was not the question Jesus asked as he made his pilgrimage here on earth. Jesus didn't wander the earth thinking, *What is the least I can do and still save this miserable lot?* Jesus, the personification of the lover, asks, What is the most I can do?

I don't know how often you should pray the Rosary. There are some people who think everyone should pray the Rosary every day. In my own life, there have been months, even years, when I have prayed the Rosary every day. At other times, I have gone weeks and months without praying it. Generally I have discovered that when I make time for this simple but profound practice of prayer, I am a better person. When I have the discipline to pray the Rosary regularly, I seem to have a certain calmness and a heightened awareness, which makes me more readily disposed to living a life of virtue.

I don't think we need to enter the debate of whether every Catholic should pray the Rosary every day. I do, however, think that all Catholics should be able to bring forth the Rosary from their spiritual storehouse from time to time as the Spirit prompts them.

Our spiritual lives should be dynamic. Our love should be constant, but it may express itself in many different ways at different times. So it is with prayer. Learn to allow the Spirit to guide you to the type of prayer that will most benefit you during a particular season in your life. Not the type of prayer you "feel like" doing, but the type of prayer that will most benefit you that day, week, month, year, or decade, depending on what is happening in your life, the disposition of your soul, and what great work God is trying to do in you and through you.

FINDING THE DEEP PLACE WITHIN

I am fascinated with one particular line about Mary in the Gospel of Luke. Mary and Joseph had brought Jesus to the temple for the official ritual, the presentation of the child to God. There was a man named Simeon in the temple that day.

He was often there, it seems. He was a holy man, or a prophet, or a mystic—perhaps all three. He cried out in prayer, praising the child as the Messiah and praising God for letting him live long enough for the coming of the Messiah. Then he spoke with Mary about what her son was going to do, what was going to happen to her son, and how it was going to impact her. After the Gospel retells this story, we read this beautiful and simple line: "But Mary treasured all these words, and pondered them in her heart" (Luke 2:19).

I've always wondered, how much did Mary know? And when did she know it? When the angel Gabriel appeared to her, did God infuse her with a complete vision of Jesus' life? Were those nine months while Jesus was in her womb an intense mystical university? Did she know what was coming? Did she just know that her son was the chosen one? Or did she have to watch his life unfold like everyone else?

Mary pondered the words of Simeon in her heart. When was the last time you treasured any words? When did you last ponder deep in your heart something that happened to you?

Ours is a culture of hyper-gossip. We live in the age of social media mania, and so we are tempted to blurt out every happening and thought instantly. Is this just another form of gossip? If people could post events before they happened, they would. So many cannot wait to post online all the details of their lives. This leads to shallow relationships, which lead in turn to shallow lives.

Are you able to know things and not tell others? Are you able to hold on to some of your experiences and ponder them in your heart?

All prayer is an invitation to ponder. This is especially true for the Rosary because it leads so naturally to pondering.

•••••••

When I was thirteen years old, Pope John Paul II came to Australia. My father took me to the Pope's Mass. It was outdoors, and there were a lot of people. We were far away from the pope, but there were huge screens that allowed us to see clearly everything that was happening.

After Communion the pope knelt to pray on a kneeler that was directly in front of the altar. I saw him kneel and close his eyes, and even as a teen I knew I was in the presence of a spiritual master. I wouldn't have used those words back then, but I think that was the first time in my life I had ever seen someone really pray. He knelt down, closed his eyes, and even with my limited spiritual development, I could tell he was going to a deep place. I mean deep, deep, deep. You don't see that very often. On Sunday when you are returning to your pew, you rarely see someone absorbed in prayer.

It took me a couple of years to get serious about it, but I went off in search of that deep place. It has been the greatest adventure of my life. I wish I could relive those early days again, but like so many things, nothing compares to the first time you discover that deep contemplation is possible even for you.

This is what I would like to say to you above all: Find that deep place within you. To live your whole life and never find it would be a tragedy. To find that deep place and not spend time there each day would be absurd.

Find that deep place within, and start to live your life from that deep place. Spend time there with God every day. Allow him to show you who you are, what you're here for, what matters most, and what matters least. Make the decisions of your life in that deep place based on what God teaches you there.

Find that deep place where you can connect with God and with the-best-version-of-yourself, a place where you can rest with God and then burst forth into the world to carry out the mission he has placed in your heart.

Reject the shallow. Learn to ponder. Learn to think deeply.

Our world has become shallow, superficial, thoughtless, and unthinking. In the midst of that, God is inviting you to live a life of contemplation; he is inviting you to think, and think deeply, about the things we've discussed, but also about the ordinary things of everyday life. Be mindful not to let your contemplation lead you into isolation. Any authentic experience should lead us deeper and deeper into relationship with God, but also with our neighbor.

The world needs brave men and women who will do the work to find that deep place, where they can experience union with God and live their lives from that mystical place. The Rosary will help you to find that place, and it is a great way to spend time with God there.

Don't be afraid of the deep waters. It is only in the deep waters that we find the great catch (see Luke 5:6) that we are all yearning for from the moment we are born.

A little depth in this shallow world is good for the soul.

PRAYERLESSNESS: THE CURSE OF OUR AGE

Prayerlessness is one of the great torments of modern times. For decades the time we spend in focused prayer has been diminishing as our lives have become busier and busier. We have fallen into the tyranny of the urgent, which demands that we rush from one urgent thing to the next. The problem with this is that the most important things are hardly ever urgent. This can leave us always doing urgent things but never doing important things. It is these most important things that we never get around to in this cycle. Prayer is one of those important things, and among the highest priority. Prayer helps us to identify what matters most and strengthens our hearts and minds to give priority to those things in our daily lives. What could be more important than prayer?

Prayerlessness also distorts the human person. Without prayer, over time we forget the attitudes and qualities that make us uniquely human (compassion, generosity, humility, fortitude), and we become more and more like mere animals.

Prayer leads us to catch a glimpse of the-best-version-of-ourselves, and it helps us to develop the virtue necessary to celebrate our best selves. If you watch the evening news tonight, you will discover that the world desperately needs men and women of prayer and virtue. People in your neighborhood need your prayers, your parish needs your prayers, and your colleagues at work need your prayers. And it is painfully obvious at times that the Catholic Church is in desperate need of prayer.

Personal prayer is essential to the Christian life, but so is communal prayer. I have tried to do life on my own without God and prayer and have come to the conclusion that I would rather walk across hot coals each morning than live without prayer. Personal prayer is a deepening of your relationship with God, discovering who he is calling you to be for him and for others. The liturgical prayer of Sunday Mass is the prayer of the whole Church gathered as a public proclamation of who we are as Catholics. What you bring to Mass on Sunday is your prayer life, and the deeper it is, the more deeply you can enter into the public expression of the faith of the Church. The Mass is not simply about you; it is the whole Church gathered as a sign of hope to the world. A community at prayer is a beautiful thing.

The research project that explored what leads people to become highly engaged Catholics gave birth to *The Four Signs of a Dynamic Catholic*. The first sign of a Dynamic Catholic is prayer. Dynamic Catholics are first and foremost men and women of prayer, just as the saints were. Is it enough for us just to pray? No. We have been given the mission to transform the world. But the best action springs forth from a vibrant prayer life. Our efforts to transform society into a more loving and just experience for all must be deeply rooted in our Christianity, and thus deeply rooted in prayer. Otherwise our Christian social efforts can become disconnected from our Christianity, and this quickly diminishes into just another form of social work. Don't get me wrong—social work is good, but we are called to more than that.

I encourage you to begin (or renew) your commitment to a life of prayer today. Use the Rosary and The Prayer Process to guide you. If you do, I am confident that you will find them faithful guides that will lead you deeply into a lifelong friendship with God. What are you going to do in this life that will bring more satisfaction than developing a dynamic friendship with God?

One of the great moments in the life of any Christian comes when we realize, once and for all, that a life with prayer is better than a life without prayer, and when we give it a sacred place in our daily schedules.

PART
TWO

The following reflections were written to be used at the beginning of each decade while praying the Rosary. While I recommend that you read through them now, as you do, I simply encourage you to keep their purpose in mind. I hope you will return to use them as a companion in prayer sometime when you are praying the Rosary. I hope they lead you ever deeper into the events of Jesus' and Mary's lives that we ponder each time we pray the Rosary.

I am also recording an audio version of these reflections so that you and I can pray together: as you drive to work, exercise, or sit quietly in your favorite place to pray. To pray with someone else is a beautiful thing. It is one of life's most beautiful experiences.

We are called to a powerful and personal relationship with God, but we are also called to forge powerful and personal relationships with each other. There is something very powerful about praying with another person or with other people. It was praying the Rosary together in a prayer group that I first really experienced that in a powerful way.

In times past families used to pray the Rosary together after dinner. Perhaps that is a tradition worth revisiting. Have you ever prayed the Rosary with your spouse? Have you ever prayed the Rosary with one of your children (if you have children)? Have you ever prayed the Rosary with a friend?

I love praying with others. So, whether you get the audio version or not, I will be praying with you in spirit.

Please pray for me. I mean that. It is not gratuitous. Please pray for me. May your experience of the Rosary be ever fresh, never stale, and life-changing.

m.

THE TWENTY MYSTERIES OF THE ROSARY

The Five Joyful Mysteries

The Annunciation
The Visitation
The Birth of Jesus
The Presentation
Finding the Child Jesus in the Temple

The Five Luminous Mysteries

The Baptism of Jesus in the River Jordan
The Wedding Feast at Cana
The Proclamation of the Kingdom of God
The Transfiguration of Jesus
The Institution of the Eucharist

The Five Sorrowful Mysteries

The Agony in the Garden
The Scourging at the Pillar
The Crowning with Thorns
The Carrying of the Cross
The Crucifixion of Jesus

The Five Glorious Mysteries

The Resurrection
The Ascension
Pentecost
The Assumption
The Crowning of Mary Queen of Heaven

The Joyful Mysteries are typically prayed on Monday and Saturday; the Luminous Mysteries on Thursday; the Sorrowful Mysteries on Tuesday and Friday; and the Glorious Mysteries on Wednesday and Sunday.

The Joyful Mysteries

The Annunciation

Fruit of the Mystery: The Desire to Do God's Will

The Visitation

Fruit of the Mystery: Humble Service to Others

The Birth of Jesus

Fruit of the Mystery: Gratitude for Life

The Presentation

Fruit of the Mystery: Learning to Listen Deeply

Finding the Child Jesus in the Temple

Fruit of the Mystery: Wisdom

THE FIRST JOYFUL MYSTERY

The Annunciation

Fruit of the Mystery: The Desire to Do God's Will

A Reading from the Gospel of Luke

The Birth of Jesus Foretold

In the sixth month the angel Gabriel was sent from God to a city of Galilee named Nazareth, to a virgin betrothed to a man whose name was Joseph, of the house of David; and the virgin's name was Mary. And he came to her and said, "Hail, full of grace, the Lord is with you!" But she was greatly troubled at the saying, and considered in her mind what sort of greeting this might be. And the angel said to her "Do not be afraid, Mary, for you have found favor with God. And behold, you will conceive in your womb and bear a son, and you shall call his name Jesus.

"He will be great, and will be called the Son of the Most High; and the Lord God will give to him the throne of his father David, and he will reign over the house of Jacob for ever; and of his kingdom there will be no end."

And Mary said to the angel, "How can this be, since I have no husband?" And the angel said to her, "The Holy Spirit will come upon you, and the power of the Most High will overshadow you; therefore the child to be born will be called holy, the Son of God.

"And behold, your kinswoman Elizabeth in her old age has also conceived a son; and this is the sixth month with her who was called barren. For with God nothing will be impossible." And Mary said, "Behold, I am the handmaid of the Lord; let it be to me according to your word." And the angel departed from her.

Luke 1:26–38

REFLECTION

Yes. It all comes down to that in the end. Are we willing to say yes to God? There are some beautiful lines in the Scriptures that sum everything up. On the wall in my children's room is a picture of Noah's ark, and inscribed in the wooden frame are the words "Noah did all that God asked him to do" (Genesis 7:5). That's it. Just do what God asks you to do. At the wedding feast in Cana, Mary said to the servants, "Do whatever he tells you" (John 2:5). Say yes to God in everything.

One moment at a time, we are each called to embrace his will. It is monumentally simple and monumentally difficult. But we find ways to complicate and avoid it.

Why don't we passionately seek God's will? All too often I find myself saying yes to God begrudgingly. It isn't a generous yes. I know that, and I know God knows it.

Mary puts me to shame. Her humble words of surrender, "Let it be it done unto me according to your word," echo throughout history as a spirituality unto themselves: Seek and do what you believe to be the will of God.

We should be a people of yes, generously saying yes to everything God calls us to. I cannot help but think, though, of those times when I have knowingly said no to God. They sting. And yet I know Mary would take me in her arms right now, hold me, encourage me, and send me out into the world inspired anew.

Let's begin again right now—a new beginning, a fresh commitment to say yes to God. And may these words never be far from our lips: "God, what do you think I should do in this situation?"

PRAYER

With these inspirations in our hearts and minds, we turn to you, Jesus, and pray.

Lord of every yes, give us wisdom to generously say yes to your way in the moments of the day; give us courage to turn our backs on anything that is not of you, no matter how enticing it may be to our senses or our ego.

You can take and you can give. Take from us the desire for anything that doesn't help us become the-best-version-of-ourselves, and give us the desire to do your will in all things. Give us the grace to say yes to you in the big things and the small things, in old ways and in new ways.

Jesus, we offer this decade to you for our family, living and deceased, wherever they are today, physically and spiritually. We ask you to fill them with the grace to take one step closer to you today. We also pray in a special way for every woman who found out she was pregnant today, and ask you to bless her with peace and hope.

Mary, pray for us and teach us to say yes to God in all things.

Amen.

THE SECOND JOYFUL MYSTERY

The Visitation

Fruit of the Mystery: Humble Service to Others

A Reading from the Gospel of Luke

Mary Visits Elizabeth

In those days Mary arose and went with all haste into the hill country, to a city of Judah, and she entered the house of Zechariah and greeted Elizabeth. And when Elizabeth heard the greeting of Mary, the babe leaped in her womb; and Elizabeth was filled with the Holy Spirit and she exclaimed with a loud cry, "Blessed are you among women, and blessed is the fruit of your womb! And why is this granted me, that the mother of my Lord should come to me? For behold, when the voice of your greeting came to my ears, the babe in my womb leaped for joy. And blessed is she who believed that there would be a fulfillment of what was spoken to her from the Lord."

And Mary said, "My soul magnifies the Lord, and my spirit rejoices in God my Savior, for he has regarded the low estate of his handmaiden. For behold, henceforth all generations will call me blessed; for he who is mighty has done great things for me, and holy is his name. And his mercy is on those who fear him from generation to generation. He has shown strength with his arm, he has scattered the proud in the imagination of their hearts, he has put down the mighty from their thrones, and exalted those of low degree; he has filled the hungry with good things, and the rich he has sent empty away. He has helped his servant Israel, in remembrance of his mercy, as he spoke to our fathers, to Abraham and to his posterity for ever."

And Mary remained with her about three months, and returned to her home.

Luke 1:39–56

REFLECTION

When is the last time you responded to your spouse, parents, or customers "with all haste"? When your husband or wife asks you to do a chore, or when your manager at work asks you to do a little extra, do you respond with an enthusiasm to serve? We live in an age of meaninglessness, because we have lost sight of the fact that our very purpose is to serve God and others.

Mary rushed off to serve Elizabeth. It was her first reaction. Too often my first reaction is one of selfishness: "I don't feel like it"; "I'll do it later"; "Can't someone else take care of it?" But Mary had an instinct to serve, an ingrained humility.

God wants to fill us with a holy sense of urgency. Every day people are losing hope. God seems far from them. They feel forgotten, invisible, unloved. So much is at stake. Mary wants to teach us to love God and neighbor with this holy sense of urgency.

It's time to strive again to recognize God and his invitation to serve in life's ordinary moments. The Scriptures tell us that when Mary greets Elizabeth, the child John the Baptist leaps for joy in her womb. Even in the womb, John the Baptist recognizes he is in the presence of God. Too often, I get caught up in thoughts about my own needs or desires and become completely oblivious to God's presence in a situation or person.

There is a connection between this passage and an Old Testament passage in which David dances for joy before the ark of the covenant. For the Jewish people the ark of the covenant represents God's presence among them. Just as David danced for joy in the presence of God, we now see John the Baptist dancing for joy in the presence of God. At the moment, Mary was a human tabernacle ushering God into the presence of Elizabeth and John the Baptist—and their incredible awareness allowed them to recognize that astounding truth.

We have lost our senses. We have truly lost our spiritual senses. They have been dulled and drowned out by the chaos of our lives. Let's beg God to awaken and sharpen our spiritual senses so we can recognize him in every moment and dance for joy.

PRAYER

With these inspirations in our hearts and minds, we turn to you, Jesus, and pray.

Lord, fill us with a holy sense of urgency. Teach us to never put off an opportunity to share your love with others. Strip from us all complacency, laziness, and selfishness that prevent us from serving powerfully.

Inspire in us a love of service. Open our eyes and allow us to see serving others as a holy endeavor. Cast out our selfish desire to be served and replace it with a hunger to rediscover the meaning and purpose of our lives by putting others first.

Jesus, we offer this decade of the Rosary to you and your mother for our friends—past, present, and future. Reinvigorate us with the true spirit of friendship. We pray for the friends who love and encourage us today and the friends of other places and times in our lives with whom we have lost touch. We humbly ask that our prayer might give them the courage to take one step closer to you today. We also pray in a special way for all those who are lonely today and desperate for someone to visit them.

Mary, pray for us and teach us to recognize God at work in our lives.

Amen.

THE THIRD JOYFUL MYSTERY

The Birth of Jesus

Fruit of the Mystery: Gratitude for Life

A Reading from the Gospel of Luke

The Birth of Jesus
In those days a decree went out from Caesar Augustus that all the world should be enrolled. And all went to be enrolled, each to his own city. Joseph also went up from Galilee, from the city of Nazareth, to Judea, to the city of David, which is called Bethlehem, because he was of the house and lineage of David, to be enrolled with Mary, his betrothed, who was with child. And while they were there, the time came for her to be delivered. And she gave birth to her first-born son and wrapped him in swaddling cloths, and laid him in a manger, because there was no place for them in the inn.

And in that region there were shepherds out in the field, keeping watch over their flock by night. And an angel of the Lord appeared to them, and the glory of the Lord shone around them, and they were filled with fear. And the angel said to them, "Be not afraid; for behold, I bring you good news of a great joy which will come to all the people; for to you is born this day in the city of David a Savior, who is Christ the Lord. And this will be a sign for you: you will find a babe wrapped in swaddling cloths and lying in a manger." And suddenly there was with the angel a multitude of the heavenly host praising God and saying,

"Glory to God in the highest, and on earth peace among men with whom he is pleased!"

When the angels went away from them into heaven, the shepherds said to one another, "Let us go over to Bethlehem and see this thing that has happened, which the Lord has made known to us." And they went with haste, and found Mary and Joseph, and the babe lying in a manger. And when they saw it they made known the saying which had been told them concerning this child; and all who heard it wondered at what the shepherds told them. But Mary kept all these things, pondering them in her heart. And the shepherds returned, glorifying and praising God for all they had heard and seen, as it had been told them.

Luke 2:1–20

REFLECTION

I love Christmas. People are different during this season. There seems to be more of a spirit of goodwill in the world. I am different. And I try to keep the spirit of Christmas alive throughout the year, but I fail again and again.

Let's exercise our spiritual senses and imagine that tonight is the night when Jesus is born. Place yourself there in Bethlehem on that holy night. The baby Jesus is lying there in the manger, with Mary and Joseph around him.

I will imagine myself as one of the shepherds. Who will you imagine yourself as? You are even keener to be with Jesus—you are one of the wise men. You have followed the star across the face of the earth just to have a few short moments with Jesus. There is a peace and a joy that are unattainable through the things of this world, and we find it here with Mary, Joseph, and the child Jesus. We spend time with the Holy

Family. Time stands still. Have we been here for moments or for hours? How can being in their presence not change us?

As we leave, it strikes us. The world is a mess: war, poverty, corruption, greed, selfishness, violence, abuse, and injustice. The face of evil torments ordinary people every day. And God chose to put himself in the middle of our mess.

There are so many times when we try to avoid other people's messes. We judge: "It's your mess. You made it; you should clean it up." We justify: "People have to learn . . ." God's attitude is the complete opposite. He places himself right in the middle of our mess as the solution to it. We don't deserve it. We have no claim to it. God gives us a new beginning, a fresh start, freely and without merit.

PRAYER

With these inspirations in our hearts and minds, we turn to you, Jesus, and pray.

Lord, help us to be constantly aware that life is precious. Liberate us from our life-wasting habits so that we can live life to the fullest. Nudge us when we feel tempted to waste a day or an hour, or even a few minutes.

Remove any judgment from our hearts that causes us to think of ourselves as different from or better than others in any way. Warm our hearts so that we may see that it is within our power to help other people clean up their messes, and to act with the generous mercy you have shown us.

Jesus, we offer this decade to you for our own mothers—living or deceased—and for all mothers. We pray for all the children who will be born today. May they each have at least one person in their lives to teach them to walk with you. We pray in a special way for single mothers and for all those couples struggling to conceive a child, and for all parents who have lost a child.

Mary, pray for us and share your wisdom with all mothers.

Amen.

THE FOURTH JOYFUL MYSTERY

The Presentation

Fruit of the Mystery: Learning to Listen Deeply

A Reading from the Gospel of Luke

The Presentation of Jesus in the Temple
When the time came for their purification according to the law
of Moses, they brought him up to Jerusalem to present him to
the Lord (as it is written in the law of the Lord, "Every first-
born male shall be designated as holy to the Lord"), and they
offered a sacrifice according to what is stated in the law of the
Lord, "a pair of turtledoves or two young pigeons."

Now there was a man in Jerusalem whose name was Simeon; this man was righteous and devout, looking forward to the
consolation of Israel, and the Holy Spirit rested on him. It had
been revealed to him by the Holy Spirit that he would not see
death before he had seen the Lord's Messiah. Guided by the
Spirit, Simeon came into the temple; and when the parents
brought in the child Jesus, to do for him what was customary
under the law, Simeon took him in his arms and praised God,
saying,

"Master, now you are dismissing your servant in peace, according to your word; for my eyes have seen your salvation,
which you have prepared in the presence of all peoples, a
light for revelation to the Gentiles and for glory to your people Israel."

And the child's father and mother were amazed at what was
being said about him. Then Simeon blessed them and said to
his mother Mary, "This child is destined for the falling and the
rising of many in Israel, and to be a sign that will be opposed so

that the inner thoughts of many will be revealed—and a sword will pierce your own soul too."

When they had finished everything required by the law of the Lord, they returned to Galilee, to their own town of Nazareth. The child grew and became strong, filled with wisdom; and the favor of God was upon him.

Luke 2:22–35, 39–40

REFLECTION

Have you ever waited for something with great anticipation? Did you wait patiently? What are you waiting for in your life right now?

Simeon had waited. This was his moment. He had waited patiently, and he had prayed patiently. Now he took baby Jesus in his arms. Imagine the emotion as he pulled the child to his chest, his long gray beard caressing the child's head. His face filled with a strange combination of joy and anguish—joy for the present, anguish for the future he knew or sensed the child would face. The tears streaming down his face.

Put yourself there in the temple that day. Mary and Joseph have brought Jesus to present him to the Lord in obedience to the Jewish law. Mary, the Mother of God, submits her child to the Law of Moses. Think about it: They are presenting God to God, and yet they are obedient to the law. If anyone was ever exempt from a law, it was Jesus, Mary, and Joseph in this moment. But they chose obedience. This is a momentous act of humility.

How often do we decide that a particular rule or law doesn't apply to us? When we drive faster than the speed limit, neglect to declare some taxable income, or leave our phones on when we're on a plane or in a theater, we are really saying, "That law doesn't apply to me. That's for everyone else. I am above that law." This is our arrogance.

"Poverty, chastity, and obedience. Obedience is by far the hardest to live," a wise old monk once told me. To whom are you willing to be obedient? We are allergic to the very word. It seems we are obedient only to our own desires. Addicted to comfort and convenience, we reject the very notion of obedience. No wonder we have such a hard time surrendering in obedience to the will of God.

The word *obedience* comes from the Latin word *obedire*, which means "to listen deeply." Mary listened deeply. Simeon listened deeply. By listening deeply they saw the wisdom of God's way.

PRAYER

With these inspirations in our hearts and minds, we turn to you, Jesus, and pray.

Lord, give us the patience of Simeon, knowing that often our impatience gets in the way of obedience; give us the grace necessary to see obedience as something that is life-giving rather than something that is oppressive. Help us to become a little more patient each day, and light a flame of desire for obedience in our hearts.

Inspire us to realize that your guidance, rules, and laws are designed in part to protect us from the great misery people experience when they reject your wisdom. And knowing that we cannot love you if we are not obedient to you, we present ourselves to you today just as Mary and Joseph presented Jesus.

Instruct us in all things; guide us in all things; command us in all things; we desire to be your faithful servants.

Jesus, we offer this decade to you for the Church; help us together as the Church to meet people where they are and lead them to where you are calling them to be. We pray for all those involved in Catholic education, for religious orders, deacons, priests, bishops, and the pope.

We also pray in a special way for anyone who has been discouraged or hurt by the Church. We ask that you heal them by sending each and every one of them someone to love them out of their hurt.

Mary, pray for us and teach us to listen deeply to your son.

Amen.

THE FIFTH JOYFUL MYSTERY

The Finding of Jesus in the Temple

Fruit of the Mystery: Wisdom

A Reading from the Gospel of Luke

The Boy Jesus in the Temple

Now every year his parents went to Jerusalem for the festival of the Passover. And when he was twelve years old, they went up as usual for the festival. When the festival was ended and they started to return, the boy Jesus stayed behind in Jerusalem, but his parents did not know it.

Assuming that he was in the group of travelers, they went a day's journey. Then they started to look for him among their relatives and friends. When they did not find him, they returned to Jerusalem to search for him.

After three days they found him in the temple, sitting among the teachers, listening to them and asking them questions. And all who heard him were amazed at his understanding and his answers.

When his parents saw him they were astonished; and his mother said to him, "Child, why have you treated us like this? Look, your father and I have been searching for you in great anxiety." He said to them, "Why were you searching for me? Did you not know that I must be in my Father's house?" But they did not understand what he said to them.

Luke 2:41–50

REFLECTION

Have You Ever Lost Something?

When I think of Mary, I imagine someone very calm and peaceful, but now she is frantic. She is rushing from one place to another, asking people, "Have you seen Jesus?" The mild-mannered Joseph is shouting, "Jesus, Jesus!" The other people in the group become restless and disturbed; they have never seen Mary and Joseph like this either.

Think about when your wallet or your keys go missing. You panic at the possibility that they are lost or stolen, but most of the time you have just misplaced them. These are just things. Have you ever lost your child while shopping—even just lost sight of him or her for a few minutes? Your heart pounds; you feel like throwing up; you become frantic. God, the Creator of the Universe, entrusted Jesus the Messiah to Mary and Joseph's care—and they lost him. Imagine what they must have been thinking and how they were feeling: grief, torment, distress, anguish, torture.

And yet, so often we lose Jesus in our own lives and don't even notice. It might be days or weeks before we realize that we have lost him.

Word begins to spread of a boy teaching in the temple with astounding wisdom. The news reaches Mary and Joseph, and they rush to the temple. I follow them, trying to keep up, and as I enter the temple, I see you, sitting at Jesus' feet. Listening. Pondering. And with every word, he inspires you to be a better person and live a better life.

PRAYER

With these inspirations in our hearts and minds, we turn to you, Jesus, and pray.

Lord, help us to be constantly aware of your presence in our lives. Teach us to recognize you at work in the ordinary and extraordinary moments of life.

Just as it was perfectly natural for Jesus to be teaching in the synagogue, help me to find the one thing that you want me to passionately pursue. Free me of regret for lost time and fear of the future. Liberate me from the foolishness of thinking that I am too young or too old for you to work powerfully through me.

You made us for mission. You made us for service to others, and without this our lives seem empty and meaningless. Help us each to find our way to join you in ministry, whether that is greeting people warmly as they arrive at church on Sunday, starting a Bible study or a book club, or becoming a missionary in Africa, China, or right here in America.

Don't let us fall into the temptation of judging our mission and ministry. Help us to know that you have given us the perfect mix of talents and abilities to fulfill the mission you have designed for us.

Jesus, we offer this decade to you for everyone struggling to discover what exactly they should do with their lives. Give them insight and hope. And we pray in a special way for parents who have lost a child—for those whose child has died from illness or in war, been murdered or kidnapped. Ease their anguish. We pray also for those who have lost the right to see their children each day because of divorce or addiction.

Mary, pray for us and inspire in us the courage and perseverance to never stop seeking Jesus.

Amen.

The Luminous Mysteries

The Baptism of Jesus in the River Jordan

Fruit of the Mystery: Healing of Body, Mind, and Soul

The Wedding Feast at Cana

Fruit of the Mystery: Generous Hospitality

The Proclamation of the Kingdom of God

Fruit of the Mystery: Desire for Holiness

The Transfiguration of Jesus

Fruit of the Mystery: Trust in God

The Institution of the Eucharist

Fruit of the Mystery: Belief in the True Presence of Jesus in the Eucharist

THE FIRST LUMINOUS MYSTERY

The Baptism of Jesus in the River Jordan

Fruit of the Mystery: Healing of Body, Mind, and Soul

A Reading from the Gospel of Matthew

The Baptism of Jesus in the River Jordan
Jesus came from Galilee to John at the Jordan, to be baptized by him. John would have prevented him, saying, "I need to be baptized by you, and do you come to me?" But Jesus answered him, "Let it be so now; for it is proper for us in this way to fulfill all righteousness." Then he consented.

And when Jesus had been baptized, just as he came up from the water, suddenly the heavens were opened to him and he saw the Spirit of God descending like a dove and alighting on him. And a voice from heaven said, "This is my Beloved Son, with whom I am well pleased."

Matthew 3:13–17

REFLECTION

John the Baptist felt unworthy even to untie Jesus' sandals, but now Jesus stood in line with sinners and presented himself to John to be baptized. It seems to me that the more someone tries to grow spiritually, the more he or she struggles to embrace in a healthy way the unworthiness we all share. Teresa of Ávila counsels us: "Humility is truth." Jesus counsels us not to bury our talents or hide our light. Are we unworthy of God's love and infinite blessings? Yes. But that is only half the picture; the other half is that human beings are amazing and God loves us beyond comprehension.

When my first child was born, my spirituality was impacted significantly. I have always believed that God loves me. But when Walter was born, I began to experience the love of God in the very core of my soul.

I love my children more than I ever thought was possible before I had children. And here's the thing: I am weak and broken, fragile and flawed. But if I can love my children as much as I do, with all my limitations, imagine how much God loves his children—you and me!

It all makes me feel unworthy. Yes, I feel blessed, and yet I often struggle with feelings of inadequacy and unworthiness. Some of this is natural and normal, healthy and good for us. But it is so easy to go too far and forget that as sons and daughters of the great King, and as his children, despite our unworthiness, we are invited by God to participate in all that his kingdom has to offer.

PRAYER

With these inspirations in our hearts and minds, we turn to you, Jesus, and pray.

Lord of truth and order, shine that truth and order upon us today so we can have and hold an honest and healthy sense of who we are and who we are not. Help us to see ourselves as you see us.

Let our self-esteem be based not upon the things we have done or not done, nor upon the things of this world that we have or don't have, nor upon our accomplishments or failures. Let our self-esteem be based upon the love you, your Father, and the Spirit shower upon us in every moment. Let it be the quiet, joyful confidence of a child who lives under the providence and protection of a powerful father.

Jesus, we offer this decade to you and your mother for every person, adult or child, who will be baptized today. Let the new life of baptism animate them for the rest of their lives. We also pray in a special way for people who lack the clarity or courage to live out the call of their baptism today. May there be better days ahead for them.

Mary, Mother of God and mother to us all, you are the most honored woman in history. Share with us your deep humility and steadfast confidence so that we can have a healthy sense of self.

Amen.

THE SECOND LUMINOUS MYSTERY

The Wedding Feast at Cana

Fruit of the Mystery: Generous Hospitality

A Reading from the Gospel of John

The Wedding Feast at Cana

On the third day there was a wedding in Cana of Galilee, and the mother of Jesus was there. Jesus and his disciples had also been invited to the wedding.

When the wine gave out, the mother of Jesus said to him, "They have no wine." And Jesus said to her, "Woman, what concern is that to you and to me? My hour has not yet come." His mother said to the servants, "Do whatever he tells you."

Now standing there were six stone water jars for the Jewish rites of purification, each holding twenty or thirty gallons. Jesus said to them, "Fill the jars with water." And they filled them up to the brim.

He said to them, "Now draw some out, and take it to the chief steward." So they took it. When the steward tasted the water that had become wine, and did not know where it came from (though the servants who had drawn the water knew), the steward called the bridegroom and said to him, "Everyone serves the good wine first, and then the inferior wine after the guests have become drunk. But you have kept the good wine until now."

Jesus did this, the first of his signs, in Cana of Galilee, and revealed his glory; and his disciples believed in him.

John 2:1–11

REFLECTION

Hospitality has been central to Christian culture from the very beginning. The first Christians perplexed and intrigued the people of their time with their radical hospitality, which was kind and generous, loving, thoughtful, and deeply personal in a tragically impersonal culture that treated most people like livestock. The hospitality of the first Christians made people feel welcome, and that is no small thing in a world filled with people hungry for acceptance and desperate to feel that they belong.

Weddings are a lavish expression of hospitality. Jesus and Mary were at a wedding. They did not seem to be very close to the newlyweds, and yet Mary and Jesus went to extraordinary lengths to prevent the new couple and their families from suffering the embarrassment of running out of wine.

Mary took hospitality so seriously that she asked her son to alter the events of history. Jesus obviously had a plan to begin his public life in some particular way at some particular time, and this was not it, but Mary asked him to change his plans. You recall that Jesus objected, saying it was not his time, and yet he ultimately complied with his mother's request. He denied himself, died unto himself, inconvenienced himself, and allowed his mother's request to change the course of salvation history. This alone shows us the incredible respect that Jesus had for Mary.

How do you react when people ask you to change your plans (in infinitely less significant ways)?

I've been reflecting on this mystery for thirty years, but something new just occurred to me. Mary must have known that Jesus could do something. Her request assumed that Jesus could solve the problem. How did she know? What extraordinary things had Mary seen Jesus do during the first thirty years of his life?

Every day we encounter opportunities to live our faith through hospitality. My wife and I like to make people feel so welcome when they stay with us that they never want to leave. As a leader of people at work, I see the workplace as a rich opportunity for hospitality with both our employees and customers; and I see Dynamic Catholic as a rich opportunity for radical hospitality with team members, donors, and customers. Each day presents a variety of invitations to extend kind and generous hospitality toward the people who cross our paths.

Next Sunday an out-of-town visitor will walk into your parish church for Mass. Will she feel welcomed? Will she walk away wishing that she and her family lived in the area so they could go to your church every Sunday because you made her feel so welcome?

Do you feel welcome in your own parish? Would a new parishioner feel welcome? How many people do you think don't really feel welcome in their parish?

Hospitality is a powerful ministry. Jesus never preached to anyone before he had addressed some human need. First he fed them, healed them, comforted them, made them feel like they belonged and were welcome. He opened their hearts to the divine by paying attention to their ordinary human needs.

Let's make our homes and parishes temples of welcome, temples of hospitality. People hear differently, respond differently, live differently, and give differently when they feel welcome.

PRAYER

With these inspirations in our hearts and minds, we turn to you, Jesus, and pray.

Lord, you inspired the first Christians to adopt generous hospitality as a way of life. By developing a rare awareness of other people's needs, they loved you by loving each other. In the process this generous hospitality helped them to build strong marriages and families, vibrant communities, and an identity in the broader culture that fascinated people.

Enrich all marriages and families with hospitality. Make us mindful of each other's needs and eager to serve them. Lord, use hospitality to renew marriage in our society. It is a practical and profound way to put the needs of others before our own. It demonstrates with action each day that we love each other. Inspire each marriage to become one of generous hospitality.

Jesus, we offer this decade to you for all married couples around the world; help them to appreciate each other. Give them courage to talk about the things that are difficult to talk about so their marriages can continue to grow.

We also pray in a special way for all couples getting married today; may the hope and joy of this day live on throughout their marriage. We pray for all engaged couples; give them the wisdom to prepare for marriage and not just plan a wedding. We pray also for those married couples celebrating their anniversary today, and we pray for any couple struggling in their marriage right now. We hold up to you all those who have suffered and continue to suffer the effects of divorce—the men, the women, and most especially the children.

Finally, Jesus, we ask that just as you abundantly supplied more wine when it was in short supply at the wedding in Cana, please provide abundantly for whatever is in short supply in our lives today.

Mary, in Cana you displayed the awareness of hospitality. Help us to become more aware every single day of what is happening within us and around us. Especially increase our awareness of the needs of others.

Amen.

THE THIRD LUMINOUS MYSTERY

The Proclamation of the Kingdom of God
Fruit of the Mystery: Desire for Holiness

A Reading from the Gospel of Matthew

Jesus Proclaims the Kingdom of God
When Jesus saw the crowds, he went up the mountain; and after he sat down, his disciples came to him. Then he began to speak, and taught them, saying:

> "Blessed are the poor in spirit, for theirs is the kingdom of heaven.
> "Blessed are those who mourn, for they will be comforted.
> "Blessed are the meek, for they will inherit the earth.
> "Blessed are those who hunger and thirst for righteousness, for they will be filled.
> "Blessed are the merciful, for they will receive mercy.
> "Blessed are the pure in heart, for they will see God.
> "Blessed are the peacemakers, for they will be called children of God.
> "Blessed are those who are persecuted for righteousness' sake, for theirs is the kingdom of heaven.

> "Blessed are you when people revile you and persecute you and utter all kinds of evil against you falsely on my account. Rejoice and be glad, for your reward is great in heaven, for in the same way they persecuted the prophets who were before you."

Matthew 5:1–11

REFLECTION

When Jesus spoke about the kingdom, he perplexed people. They had a certain image of God and his ways, and Jesus turned it upside down and inside out. In our own ways, we too have images of God and ways of thinking about how he does things that he wants to turn upside down—which, as it turns out, will be right side up.

The kingdom is different. God's ways are not man's ways. The first will be last. All men, women, and children are equal—the rich and the poor, the healthy and the sick, the young and the old. The world lusts for power and might, while the kingdom of God is ruled by truth, beauty, and goodness. The currency of a worldly kingdom is money and influence, but the currency of God's kingdom is kindness, compassion, and mercy. The world seeks control; God loves freedom. The world is motivated by self-interest, while the kingdom of God invites us to set aside our own interests to pursue the will of God and lay down our life for others. The world worships possessions and accomplishments; the kingdom says who you become is infinitely more important than what you do or what you have. The world seeks ever more; the kingdom says less is more. The world complicates; the kingdom simplifies. The world lusts, while the kingdom loves. The world confuses, but the kingdom clarifies. The world hates enemies; the kingdom has no enemies because we love our enemies until they become one with us. The world is divided; the kingdom is united.

The kingdom of God looks and acts like Jesus. It is a kingdom of outrageous generosity.

Everyone needs the kingdom. It's a place; it's a person; it's a worldview; it's the question and the answer; it's the ultimate system of values. And it is to be sought unrelentingly.

Jesus came to reveal the kingdom of God to us so we could live loving and just lives in the eyes of God. He stays at our side, encouraging and challenging us, so that we can live up to the promise of baptism, live more loving and just lives, and in the process make our tiny corner of the world more loving and just.

Jesus invites us to live in this world in a kingdom way. Is your life making the world more like the kingdom of God? How are you proclaiming the kingdom of God in your own life?

PRAYER

With these inspirations in our hearts and minds, we turn to you, Jesus, and pray.

Lord of this world and the next, help us to see this world for what it is and open our spiritual senses to see the next world as it is: something worth living and dying for.

Give us the courage to join you in the mission to bring about the reign of your kingdom here on earth as it is in heaven. Inspire each of us in our way to see our vocation as a way to bring your love and justice to each and every situation in our lives. Give us courage when courage is needed. Give us clear thinking and compelling words when clear thinking and compelling words are needed. Give us silence when silence is needed. Give us humility when others seek to humiliate us and the kingdom. Remind us daily that it is impossible to help you build your kingdom when we are so obsessed with building our own.

Rearrange our priorities around your kingdom's priorities. Give us kingdom values, and inspire us to live them. Teach us a kingdom way of doing things, and let our goals be kingdom goals.

Jesus, we offer this decade to you for anyone actively seeking his or her mission in life. Let these people hear your voice in their lives more clearly today than ever before. We pray for those who are confused about how they should live their lives. Give them the grace of light and the wisdom of patience and free them from the devil of inaction.

We also pray in a special way for the mentally ill. We beg you to soothe their minds, bodies, and souls so they may find relief from their troubles. Give those who care for them comfort and patience. Their roles are difficult, emotionally draining, require long hours, and are often thankless; send others into their lives to thank and appreciate them.

Mary, teach us to love the kingdom and embrace kingdom values; increase our desire for the kingdom to reign in every situation, in our thoughts and actions, in our hearts, minds, souls, and lives.

Amen.

THE FOURTH LUMINOUS MYSTERY

The Transfiguration

Fruit of the Mystery: Trust in God

A Reading from the Gospel of Luke

The Transfiguration of Jesus
Now about eight days after these sayings Jesus took with him Peter and John and James, and went up on the mountain to pray. And while he was praying, the appearance of his face changed, and his clothes became dazzling white.

Suddenly they saw two men, Moses and Elijah, talking to him. They appeared in glory and were speaking of his departure, which he was about to accomplish at Jerusalem.

Now Peter and his companions were weighed down with sleep; but since they had stayed awake, they saw his glory and the two men who stood with him.

Just as they were leaving him, Peter said to Jesus, "Master, it is good for us to be here; let us make three dwellings, one for you, one for Moses, and one for Elijah"—not knowing what he said.

While he was saying this, a cloud came and overshadowed them; and they were terrified as they entered the cloud. Then from the cloud came a voice that said, "This is my Son, my Chosen; listen to him!" When the voice had spoken, Jesus was found alone. And they kept silent and in those days told no one any of the things they had seen.

Luke 9:28–36

REFLECTION

Why Moses and Elijah? Elijah represents all the prophets who yearned for the coming of Jesus. Moses is the giver of the Law. Why not Abraham, who received the promise of the Messiah and is our father in faith? One explanation is that Jesus came to fulfill the prophets and the law. The law outlined the problem of sin, and Jesus was the solution to that problem . . . and so much more.

What is the problem in your life? Are you allowing Jesus to be the solution? Are you looking at the problem from a divine perspective? Or are you looking at it from an earthly perspective and trying to solve it with your own might?

Jesus wants to show us what is possible. Too often our vision is too earthbound. He wants to open our hearts and minds to all that is possible, far beyond our limited thinking.

God is constantly trying to help us see things as they really are. The disciples, like you and I, could see Jesus only in a very limited way because of their limits. Jesus took Peter, John, and James up on the mountain so God the Father could open their spiritual eyes wider than ever before and help them see Jesus in all his glory.

God is also constantly trying to help us to see possibilities that we don't see because of our blind spots, low self-esteem, attachment to a particular path or outcome, and other flaws and limitations. Most of the time we don't see many of the options and possibilities that exist for us in a situation.

Most people have many more options than they see when making choices. We settle so easily on one or two options and then think the great dilemma is to decide between the two. But the reality is that there may be a dozen more that we are not yet aware of, because we lack the patience necessary to take inventory of all the options available to us in that situation. Sometimes we will agonize about it and sincerely struggle to choose between the two, when in truth what God is really inviting us to didn't even make our list of options because we were in too much of a rush. You always have more options than you think you do.

How would your priorities change if you saw yourself as you really are? How would you live differently?

God wants you to see things differently. He wants you to see all that you are capable of doing, being, and becoming. With this new sense of yourself, he wants you to live differently.

PRAYER

With these inspirations in our hearts and minds, we turn to you, Jesus, and pray.

Lord of possibilities, open our physical and spiritual eyes to see all the opportunities before us in every situation. Lord, help us to really see. Nudge us when we are tempted to limit ourselves and settle for less than who you made us to be. Remove the blind spots of ego, fear, ambition, prejudice, and bias, and help us to see things as they really are—and as they truly can be. Transform us into people of possibility.

Now that we are ablaze with a sense of all that is possible, help us to realize what Leon Bloy observed: "The only real sadness, the only real failure, the only great tragedy in life, is not to become a saint." In every moment of every day, remind us, Lord, that holiness is possible. And give us the courage to collaborate with you to transform each moment of life into a holy moment.

Jesus, we offer this decade of the Rosary for everyone enduring much greater problems and challenges than our own. Give them comfort, and give us compassion.

We also pray in a special way for the quiet and anonymous saints in the world who go about their days bringing joy, hope, and comfort to everyone who crosses their path. At times they too must experience discouragement and disappointment. At those times, send someone to encourage them and fill them with your energy and enthusiasm for life once more. Thank you for their example of holiness in the world. They remind us that holiness is indeed possible for ordinary people. Mary, help us to see your son as he really is, was, and ever will be.

Amen.

THE FIFTH LUMINOUS MYSTERY

The Institution of the Eucharist

Fruit of the Mystery: Belief in the True Presence
of Jesus in the Eucharist

A Reading from the Gospel of Luke

The Institution of the Eucharist

When the hour came, he took his place at the table, and the apostles with him. He said to them, "I have eagerly desired to eat this Passover with you before I suffer; for I tell you, I will not eat it until it is fulfilled in the kingdom of God."

Then he took a cup, and after giving thanks he said, "Take this and divide it among yourselves; for I tell you that from now on I will not drink of the fruit of the vine until the kingdom of God comes."

Then he took a loaf of bread, and when he had given thanks, he broke it and gave it to them, saying, "This is my body, which is given for you. Do this in remembrance of me." And he did the same with the cup after supper, saying, "This cup that is poured out for you is the new covenant in my blood.

"But see, the one who betrays me is with me, and his hand is on the table. For the Son of Man is going as it has been determined, but woe to that one by whom he is betrayed!"

Then they began to ask one another which one of them it could be who would do this.

Luke 22:14–23

REFLECTION

What We Don't Know

Indifference toward the Eucharist is one of the marks of our age. It is so easy to become indifferent—toward people, toward things of great value, and even indifferent toward life itself. It's human nature. If we do not intentionally and proactively foster the awe and respect that God, the Church, the Mass, the Eucharist, and life deserve, our hearts will become indifferent to these treasures.

Observe the attitude and behavior of Catholics at Mass, and the only conclusion you can reach is that they are indifferent toward Jesus, the Son of the living God, the King of Kings and Lord of Lords, the beginning and the end, the God-man who died for them on the cross and saved them from their sins—the same Jesus who shows us all how to be reasonably happy in this life and invites us to join him in the supreme happiness of eternity.

We live in an age of indifference. We shouldn't be surprised. If people en masse can be indifferent toward Jesus, nobody is safe from their prideful indifference.

Have you ever helped somebody, really gone above and beyond to make his life better, but then afterward he resented you? His indifference toward you stings at first, but as you reflect on all you did for him, the pain goes way beyond a shallow sting; it goes deep to the core of your heart and soul. You are shocked and appalled, but you shouldn't be. We all do it. Worst of all, we do it to God.

In a culture of indifference, nothing is holy. This is what we see in the way people speak to and treat each other, in the way anyone or anything that is good and holy is attacked.

The Mass and the Eucharist should inspire awe and a deep respect. I admit that they often don't for me. That is proof of my ignorance. The Mass and the Eucharist are ever-fresh, ever-new fountains of wisdom, love, mercy, and grace. We could go to Mass every day of our lives, and there would still be an infinite number of lessons we could learn from the Mass and the Eucharist.

One reason for our indifference is that this cynical world has dulled our spiritual senses. Our spiritual imagination and spiritual sight have both been accosted by the subtle and not-so-subtle daily attacks of our culture.

Do you know what happened at the Last Supper? If we consider this question, most of us would say yes and then recite the facts and mechanics of that historic experience. In our arrogant foolishness we think we know what happened at the Last Supper.

Let's consider what we don't know about the Last Supper. Who arrived first? Who was the last to leave? Which disciple was most concerned that the others had what they needed? What were Andrew and Peter talking about that night? What was Judas thinking as he prepared to betray his brothers and his God? Were the disciples talking about the future, making plans that would never materialize because in a matter of hours the world would change forever? Were they arguing about something trivial or inconsequential? How did that make Jesus feel, knowing what he knew about what was about to happen? Which of the disciples had the best sense of humor? Were they joking around that night before dinner, oblivious to the fact that they were about to experience one of the most serious events in the history of the world? Did they know that future generations would be able to consume the body and blood of Jesus? Did they know that people would kill and be killed over this single idea, that it would be the solitary truth that would cause so many to abandon Jesus?

Do you know what happened at the Last Supper? What we don't know about it dwarfs what we do know. What we don't know about God makes what we do know about him look like a grain of sand in the Sahara.

Let us beg Jesus to awaken our spiritual senses so that as we read the Scriptures we can smell the dust rising from the road, hear the whispers in the crowd as he speaks, notice the looks on various people's faces, and hear his words without the noise and distractions of this world.

It's amazing what we choose to focus on in our lives. It's astounding what we choose to care about. Put whatever you are worried about right now in the big picture of God, life, the history of the world, and eternity. The things we choose to make important often reveal our distorted priorities.

Indifference is a destroyer of love. Indifference often prevents love from beginning, for it places us inside an impregnable shell of uncaring.

PRAYER

With these inspirations in our hearts and minds, we turn to you, Jesus, and pray.

Lord, draw us nearer to you than ever before. Inspire us to spend time with you before the tabernacle. When the opportunity is available to spend time with you in adoration, let us embrace it. We also ask you to arrange things so that we can attend Mass more often and receive you—body, blood, soul, and divinity—in the humble host.

Banish indifference from our hearts and our lives.

Fill us today with a whole new love and respect for the power of the Eucharist. Lord, take our minuscule understanding of what the Eucharist is and what it can do to a whole new level. Somehow, somewhere, sometime, let this great divider unite all Christians and the whole world in peace and tranquility.

Jesus, we offer this decade to you for priests: for every priest who is, for every priest who has been, and for every priest who will be. Bless them, Lord, with grace unimaginable to carry out their work. Never let them doubt the importance of their work and the difference it makes for ordinary people who seek to love you, do your will, and live good lives. Lift them up when they are discouraged. Raise up in them a deep desire to heal your people, and teach them to take care of their bodies and souls just as you did.

We also pray in a special way for all those who are preparing to be priests and to minister to your people, for all those who are discerning a call to the priesthood—please give them courage. And for any priest, or any person, who has lost faith in your true presence in the Eucharist, give each of them new energy for life and ministry and new courage to share your love and your message with others.

Lord, help us to realize what we are really hungry for in our lives today, and give us the wisdom to realize that you want to feed our deepest needs with the Eucharist.

Mary, just as the priest prays, "O Priest of God, pray this Mass as if it were your first Mass, your last Mass, your only Mass," help us to approach each Mass with great respect and wonder, as if it were our first Mass, our last Mass, our only Mass.

Amen.

The Sorrowful Mysteries

The Agony in the Garden

Fruit of the Mystery: Sorrow for Sin

The Scourging at the Pillar

Fruit of the Mystery: Compassion

The Crowning with Thorns

Fruit of the Mystery: Patience

The Carrying of the Cross

Fruit of the Mystery: Courage to Face Injustice

The Crucifixion of Jesus

Fruit of the Mystery: Redemption

THE FIRST SORROWFUL MYSTERY

The Agony in the Garden

Fruit of the Mystery: Sorrow for Sin

A Reading from the Gospel of Matthew

Jesus Prays in the Garden of Gethsemane
Then Jesus went with them to a place called Gethsemane; and he said to his disciples, "Sit here while I go over there and pray."

He took with him Peter and the two sons of Zebedee, and began to be grieved and agitated. Then he said to them, "I am deeply grieved, even to death; remain here, and stay awake with me."

And going a little farther, he threw himself on the ground and prayed, "My Father, if it is possible, let this cup pass from me; yet not what I want but what you want."

Then he came to the disciples and found them sleeping; and he said to Peter, "So, could you not stay awake with me one hour? Stay awake and pray that you may not come into the time of trial; the spirit indeed is willing, but the flesh is weak."

Again he went away for the second time and prayed, "My Father, if this cannot pass unless I drink it, your will be done." Again he came and found them sleeping, for their eyes were heavy. So leaving them again, he went away and prayed for the third time, saying the same words. Then he came to the disciples and said to them, "Are you still sleeping and taking your rest? See, the hour is at hand, and the Son of Man is betrayed into the hands of sinners. Get up, let us be going. See, my betrayer is at hand."

Matthew 26:36–46

REFLECTION

You and I are there, in the garden with Jesus. The sky is dark but clear, and the air is crisp. Imagine for this meditation that you and I are two of Jesus' disciples, just a stone's throw away from him, but we grow weary and fall asleep. When Jesus comes back and wakes us, we are ashamed of ourselves. We feel weak and regretful. Jesus doesn't make us feel this way; we make ourselves feel these things.

Stay awake. He says it three times. But we cannot. We let him down. Imagine how alone he feels this night in the garden. We have added to his intense aloneness by not being able to even keep watch during these last hours with him.

Has anything changed today?

I still fall asleep today. Sometimes I fall asleep when I am praying. Perhaps Jesus is speaking to me through that experience and telling me I need more rest. But I sense he is more likely saying to me, "Why did you put your prayer off all day until the afternoon or evening?" or "Shouldn't you give prayer your best time and your best energy?" He has mentioned these things to me so many times before, and naturally I am disappointed in myself that he has to tell me once more. So I make a resolution to give prayer more priority in my life.

I fall asleep in other ways too. Some days I fall asleep in my marriage, or as a parent. There are times when I have been asleep for weeks or months with regard to physical fitness. It's so easy to take a nap from financial responsibility. God instructs us, as pilgrims who are just passing through this place we call earth, to stay awake and be constantly vigilant and attentive to what matters most, rather than letting what matters least take over our schedules and lives.

It is so easy to judge the disciples for falling asleep after Jesus specifically asked them to stay awake to pray and watch with him. In the Gospels Jesus went off to pray alone often. Perhaps the disciples thought it was just another one of those times, not realizing that this time was different, not knowing that this would be the last time.

And don't we all fall asleep in different ways in our lives when God is calling us to stay awake and be mindful of everything that is going on around us and within us?

Have you ever been in agony—physical, spiritual, emotional, psychological? Multiply that by infinity and take it to the depths of eternity, and you may get a small glimpse of what Jesus was experiencing that night in the Garden of Gethsemane.

When was the last time you spent an hour in prayer? It might be time again.

PRAYER

With these inspirations in our hearts and minds, we turn to you, Jesus, and pray.

Lord, in the garden that night you prayed openly and honestly to the Father with so much intensity that you began to sweat blood. I suppose it all comes down to the fact that you knew what was at stake. Too often I forget what is at stake.

It is impossible to ignore that I put you there in that garden that night. This realization ignites a set of emotions that begin with shame and embarrassment and end with sheer horror. You are paying for the careless debts I have amassed. My stomach turns when I consider that this is just the beginning of your total surrender to redeem me, my friends and family, colleagues at work, childhood schoolmates . . . and all of humanity.

I want to look away, run away, but I can't. You are sweating blood, and I know this is only the beginning. Nobody has even laid a hand on you yet. The anguish of all that has been and will be causes even you to wonder if there could be another way.

Worst of all, I struggle some days to even be sorry for some of my sins. There are still areas of my life that I don't surrender to you or even allow you to enter. Why don't I trust you more? Why don't I believe that everything is better done your way?

The ugly truth is that I love some of my sins. I don't want to give those particular sins up. I plan my days around them. Lord of everything that is good, true, and beautiful, help me to see that your way is the best way in all things—and help me then to give up the sins I love.

This scares me. I am certain there will be slips and falls, disappointments and failures. So first, give me desire. Give me the desire to be sorry for my sins and the desire to give up the sins I refuse to give up. Let that desire grow stronger and stronger every time I do anything kind, generous, thoughtful, or compassionate for anyone. In this way I can collaborate with you to get that flame of desire to burn like a raging fire in my heart and soul.

Jesus, we offer this decade to you for everyone around the world praying the Rosary today. Allow us to see with clarity what you are calling us to next, and give us the courage to carry it out day by day.

Mary, Mother of the same Jesus who was arrested in the garden; the same Jesus who did not resist their unjust arrest; the same Jesus who will suffer and die to renew our relationship with God; whisper in our ear each time we are tempted to sin. Whisper words of wisdom and encouragement, whisper to us the reality of the next world, so we can turn our backs on sin and strive evermore to live a life of virtue.

Amen.

THE SECOND SORROWFUL MYSTERY

The Scourging at the Pillar

Fruit of the Mystery: Compassion

A Reading from the Gospel of John

Jesus Is Scourged
Then Pilate took Jesus and had him flogged.

John 19:1

REFLECTION

One sentence. "Then Pilate took Jesus and had him flogged."
Eight words. But this would have been enough to kill most people. The flesh on his back was torn in a hundred places, blood
dripping from each small piece of his divine body ripped off
and scattered on the floor—the body of Christ. Still, this was
almost nothing compared to what he was to go through.

Why are we so cruel to each other? There is a cruel streak
that runs through humanity. You can see it in small children
playing together on the playground. They will ignore or ex-
clude another child, push another child around and laugh
about it, or insult a child by calling him names or by making
fun of what he is wearing.

Adults are often no better. Our insecurities result in cruelty toward others in many ways: gossip, exclusion, arguing
unnecessarily, negative humor, defamation, bullying. These
are just some of the everyday ways we human beings are cruel
to each other. A cursory examination of history or the crimes

committed in any city each week shows that our capacity to be cruel to each other has no bounds. This cruelty demands that we objectify the person we are being cruel to in some way, to think of him or her as less than fully human.

And yet, while we each have an overwhelming desire to be treated as a unique human being, we often ignore other people's humanity and treat them according to the function they play in our lives. Do you treat the person who serves you at a restaurant as a person or as a server? Ever wonder what is going on in that person's life? His grades might be suffering because he has to work so many hours just to pay for school and doesn't have enough time to study. She might have just had a miscarriage. He might have just found out that his dad has cancer. But most of all, like we all do from time to time, she might just be having a bad day for no particular reason. Functionalizing people—treating them according to their function instead of treating them as human beings—is a subtle and cunning form of cruelty.

Jesus didn't functionalize people. That's why we find so many people from the fringes of society at the center of so many Gospel stories. He didn't treat the prostitute like a prostitute; he treated her like a unique human being made in the image of God. He didn't reduce the tax collector to his function and treat him like a tax collector. He didn't treat the Samaritan like a Samaritan. He didn't treat the adulterer like an adulterer. He didn't treat the thief like a thief.

Jesus didn't think of the man who was scourging him as a cruel and angry beast. He thought of him as a human being, uniquely and wonderfully made. He saw the whole picture. He saw him perhaps as a desperate man trapped in a brutal system, trying to support his wife and children, struggling to survive in a culture that was harsh, impersonal, and cruel—especially to those with no power, money, rank, or position.

Now consider this: Who is the one person you have loved more than any other in your life? Jesus loved the man who scourged him more than that. Jesus loved that man more than you and I have ever loved anyone.

PRAYER

With these inspirations in our hearts and minds, we turn to you, Jesus, and pray.

Lord, teach me to love like you. There are so many obstacles that get in the way of loving like you: my selfishness and insecurities; my pride and unwillingness to forgive; my anger and envy; my lust and gluttony; my greed and laziness. Fill me with the grace to pray and fast more than ever before in my life, and cast these obstacles aside so that each day I can love more and more like you.

Help me to never judge, objectify, or functionalize people, but to see each and every person whose path I cross as you see them.

Jesus, we offer this decade to you for the man who scourged you at the pillar long ago and far away. We pray for anyone who feels trapped in a way of life that is self-destructive, sinful, and hurtful to others. Lord of liberty, open a door, break a window, dig a tunnel, crash through a wall, construct a bridge, part the sea, build a road . . . and lead each and every one of these trapped souls to a new and better life. Give them hope and fulfill that hope. We will help; just show us how.

We also pray in a special way for anyone who has been unjustly accused and punished for something they didn't do. Raise them above these painful circumstances and somehow keep their hearts from hardening with anger and resentment.

Hold them in your arms and comfort them in ways beyond human imagination. Stir the conscience of anyone who can set matters right so that justice can be celebrated no matter how long it has been.

Mary, model of patience, our impatience prevents us from loving people as we could and should. Teach us uncommon and extraordinary patience so that we can love every person in every situation as you and your son did and do.

Amen.

THE THIRD SORROWFUL MYSTERY

The Crowning with Thorns
Fruit of the Mystery: Patience

A Reading from the Gospel of Matthew

Jesus Is Mocked
Then the soldiers of the governor took Jesus into the governor's headquarters, and they gathered the whole cohort around him. They stripped him and put a scarlet robe on him, and after twisting some thorns into a crown, they put it on his head. They put a reed in his right hand and knelt before him and mocked him, saying, "Hail, King of the Jews!" They spat on him, and took the reed and struck him on the head.

Matthew 27:27–30

REFLECTION

It seems we will do anything to avoid pain and suffering today. But not Jesus. He embraced every experience of pain and suffering. Why the great difference between God's approach and the world's approach?

The world believes that suffering is meaningless and should be avoided at all costs. God believes that suffering has value. If suffering has no value, then it is such a waste of life, but if it does have value, the waste is even greater if we don't channel it toward some higher purpose.

They crowned him with thorns and used a stick to smack the crown down on his head, driving the thorns deep into his scalp. He felt it all. He accepted it all. He embraced it all. He allowed each thorn, each taunt to strengthen his resolve to do what was before him on that day when the world went dark and cold.

We don't need to go looking for suffering. There is enough inevitable and unavoidable suffering in our lives. But let's start learning from this suffering, allowing it to be a source of spiritual growth.

There is a whole continuum of suffering. At one end you have something as common as inconvenience. At the other end you have something as horrible as the death of a child. By going deep into the smaller forms rather than running from them, by embracing the lesser forms of unavoidable suffering, we allow this hideous aspect of life to strengthen our will so we can choose what is good, true, and right in the moments of our lives—but this spiritual practice of embracing suffering prepares us for greater suffering that may be in our future.

Long before Jesus was arrested in the Garden of Gethsemane, he had been preparing for all that his arrest set in motion. For thirty years before the wedding in Cana, he had been preparing for the end. Throughout his public life, he suffered in ways we will never know, and it all prepared him for fifteen hours that began with his arrest and ended with his death. Jesus being arrested and humiliated, scourged at the pillar, and crowned with thorns were small compared to what was ahead—and yet, these things prepared him and strengthened him spiritually to fully carry out his mission.

This is the Savior of the world. Look how we treated him. We ignored him, humiliated him, mocked him, scourged his flesh, spat on him, drove thorns into the tender skin around his head—but we were not finished yet.

The crown of thorns driven into his head—I did that. This is not pious talk; I know it to be true. My personal actions led to his personal suffering.

And we do it again today. With our thoughts, words, actions, or inaction, we do it again today—and not only to Jesus, but to others. Why? This is the great unspoken truth: because we love this world, we love some of our sins, and we are addicted to comfort. We love these things more than God, more than ourselves, and more than the people we love the most.

Have you ever known somebody who really changed his or her life? It doesn't happen very often. People will change in small ways, or even overhaul one aspect of their lives. But Jesus is inviting us to a radical transformation. Most people don't believe it is possible or that they are capable. Show them. Why don't you be the one to show them it is possible?

PRAYER

With these inspirations in our hearts and minds, we turn to you, Jesus, and pray.

Lord, you suffered so that we might have life and have it to the fullest. Fill us with a deep gratitude for all you have done for us, and inspire us to show our gratitude by actually living life to the fullest.

Just as you suffered so we could have a more abundant life, fill us with a desire to make sacrifices so others can live more fully. Liberate us from our attachment to comfort so we can help others live in the dignity of work, with a home that is clean and safe, and food to nourish mind, body, and soul. If giving up some of our comfort is enough to bring real dignity to others who are on the fringes of society, why are we waiting?

Lord, help us to stop confusing our wants with needs. Help us to realize that there is an order to all you do. Help us to see clearly that needs are primary and wants are secondary—whether those needs are our own or somebody else's.

Jesus, we offer this decade to you for anyone who suffers unnecessarily—physically, mentally, or spiritualty. Give us the courage to step beyond our comfort zones to do as much as we can with what we have, where we are—and to encourage others to do the same.

Mary, help us to set aside comfort and convenience occasionally and put the needs of others ahead of our wants.

Amen.

THE FOURTH SORROWFUL MYSTERY

The Carrying of the Cross

Fruit of the Mystery: Courage to Face Injustice

A Reading from the Gospels of Matthew and Luke

Jesus Is Betrayed

When Judas, his betrayer, saw that Jesus was condemned, he repented and brought back the thirty pieces of silver to the chief priests and the elders. He said, "I have sinned by betraying innocent blood." But they said, "What is that to us? See to it yourself." Throwing down the pieces of silver in the temple, he departed; and he went and hanged himself.

As they led Jesus away, they seized a man, Simon of Cyrene, who was coming from the country, and they laid the cross on him, and made him carry it behind Jesus.

A great number of the people followed him, and among them were women who were beating their breasts and wailing for him. But Jesus turned to them and said, "Daughters of Jerusalem, do not weep for me, but weep for yourselves and for your children. For the days are surely coming when they will say, 'Blessed are the barren, and the wombs that never bore, and the breasts that never nursed.' Then they will begin to say to the mountains, 'Fall on us'; and to the hills, 'Cover us.'

"For if they do this when the wood is green, what will happen when it is dry?"

Matthew 27:3–5; Luke 23:26–31

REFLECTION

The Scriptures invite us deeper and deeper into every story each time we read or ponder them. Let's consider Judas for a moment. Is he just the villain of the Gospel? Have you ever learned anything from him? Have you ever considered it from his point of view? Are you like Judas in any way?

The betrayal of Jesus by Judas is a tragedy, but not just in the obvious way. It is also a tragedy that Jesus lost one of his disciples. Imagine how much that broke Jesus' heart. Judas had been chosen to be one of the twelve who would go out and change the world.

I wonder what Judas was like in the days leading up to the betrayal. Did he start to distance himself from the other disciples? Was he visiting with old friends in Jerusalem? Did he begin to isolate himself from everyone and everything? Did he do or say anything that gave the disciples clues about what he was thinking?

They were so used to all being together. Maybe James and John thought he was with Peter and Matthew, and perhaps Peter and Matthew thought he was with some of the other disciples. So Judas may have felt all alone and may have been all alone. But why did he do it? Was Jesus just too different from his vision of the Messiah? Was he not getting enough attention? Did he feel he should have a greater leadership among the disciples? Was he exhausted from the life of ministry, seduced by the things of this world? How did Judas deceive himself?

Every sin leaves behind so many unanswered questions. Whatever the reason, Judas betrayed Jesus, broke his heart—and then killed himself and broke Jesus' heart again.

••••••

Now we are following Jesus as he carries his cross. We look at his face and deep into his eyes and wonder how he is even still alive, and he collapses. Simon of Cyrene is accosted by the guards and then helps Jesus carry his cross as if he himself were a criminal.

The Rosary is ever new because the situations and mysteries we are pondering have an unlimited number of dimensions to consider.

I wonder who made Jesus' cross. He was just doing his job, making a living to support his wife and children. Did he know it was for Jesus? How did he feel about making it? Did he feel guilty or was he completely oblivious? Or perhaps as the days and weeks went by, his role in the crucifixion led him to think about Jesus and who he really was and eventually he became a Christian. We don't know.

The point is, somebody made Jesus' cross. But it wasn't just the woodworker with his tools and hands; we made it with our sins.

PRAYER

With these inspirations in our hearts and minds, we turn to you, Jesus, and pray.

Lord, help me to carry my cross with grace and dignity, knowing that you are shouldering the burden with me.

Liberate me from selfishly seeking comfort constantly. Open my eyes spiritually so that I can see how the cross in all its forms helps me become the-best-version-of-myself.

Jesus, we offer this decade to you for anyone suffering from any form of injustice. We humans have invented so many ways to be unkind, unjust, and cruel. Help us to seek justice for ourselves and others, even when it comes at great personal cost. We also pray in a special way for the mentally ill. Many of us will never understand the cross they carry; please give us the grace to be kind and gentle with them.

Mary, what were you thinking and feeling that day? Did those images stab your heart every day for the rest of your life? Did you wake in the night sweating from the terror of reliving those moments in nightmares? Pray for us, Mary. Teach us to prayerfully endure unavoidable suffering and to comfort others when they suffer.

Amen.

THE FIFTH SORROWFUL MYSTERY

The Crucifixion of Jesus

Fruit of the Mystery: Redemption

A Reading from the Gospel of Luke

Jesus Is Crucified

Two others also, who were criminals, were led away to be put to death with him. When they came to the place that is called The Skull, they crucified Jesus there with the criminals, one on his right and one on his left. Then Jesus said, "Father, forgive them; for they do not know what they are doing." And they cast lots to divide his clothing. And the people stood by, watching; but the leaders scoffed at him, saying, "He saved others; let him save himself if he is the Messiah of God, his chosen one!" The soldiers also mocked him, coming up and offering him sour wine, and saying, "If you are the King of the Jews, save yourself!" There was also an inscription over him, "This is the King of the Jews."

One of the criminals who were hanged there kept deriding him and saying, "Are you not the Messiah? Save yourself and us!" But the other rebuked him, saying, "Do you not fear God, since you are under the same sentence of condemnation? And we indeed have been condemned justly, for we are getting what we deserve for our deeds, but this man has done nothing wrong." Then he said, "Jesus, remember me when you come into your kingdom." He replied, "Truly I tell you, today you will be with me in Paradise."

Luke 23:32–43

REFLECTION

When people stop thinking for themselves and groupthink takes control, the outcome is usually inhumane. Never was that more true than in the case of Jesus' condemnation, torture, execution, and death.

Consider the pain of a nail being driven through your wrist—just one small part of our Lord's passion. Suffering reminds us, perhaps more than anything else, that God's ways are not ours. We live in a secular culture that despises suffering as useless and proclaims that it should be avoided at all costs. As a result, pain relievers are constantly being thrust at us in the form of pills, products, experiences, and distractions.

The world has its own gospel. The message of the world is incomplete, and nothing demonstrates this incompleteness more than the world's inability to make sense of suffering. The world cannot make sense of suffering because it views suffering as worthless. The world has no answer for the inescapable, unavoidable, and inevitable suffering of our lives.

Central to this dilemma the gospel of the world faces is its inability to make sense of death. It encourages us to live in denial of death, which may be the height of the lunacy of this false gospel.

Jesus has an answer for everything. In the Old Testament Scriptures suffering is often presented as the consequence of people's sinfulness; suffering was the result of ignoring God's teachings. In some cases punishment was presented as being inflicted by God as a direct result of humanity's sinfulness. In the New Testament, Jesus boldly announces with his words and actions that suffering has value. It is a tool that can transform us into more loving people. It ushers us into higher spiritual realms. Salvation and the suffering of Jesus are inseparable. So what could be more meaningful than suffering?

What was Jesus hoping to achieve by dying on the cross? What were the dreams that gave him courage and the perseverance to go through with it? I suspect his hopes and dreams were many and beautiful. Let's consider one. He hoped his life and death would change what people placed at the center of their lives. What's at the center of your life? Money, sex, food, drugs, shopping, image, ego, and control—or the outrageous generosity, service, and love of God and neighbor that Jesus proposed?

Someone told me once that being in debt, the kind of debt you know you will never be able to pay, gives you this constant feeling like you can't breathe. There is a time and place for everything in God's plan, and every debt in the universe needs to be settled eventually. This day two thousand years ago was the time and Calvary was the place that God decided to settle our debts.

And, of course, Jesus' answer to death is resurrection, redemption, and eternal life.

PRAYER

With these inspirations in our hearts and minds, we turn to you, Jesus, and pray.

Lord, you give and take according to our needs and your wisdom. On this dark day you laid down your life to give us all a fresh start, a new beginning, and a never-ending stream of marvelous grace and beautiful mercy.

Give us the wisdom, Jesus, to use the minds you gave us to think for ourselves; teach us to develop and listen to our conscience, avoid groupthink; fill us with courage to avoid mob behavior and instead stand up for justice.

When we suffer ourselves, help us to offer that suffering to you for worthy intentions. Never let us waste our suffering by getting caught up in self-pity.

Jesus, we offer this decade to you for anyone who is suffering physically today. We ask you to fill them with the rare grace necessary to see and experience suffering as a way to get closer to you. We pray for all those we have wronged in our lives, and for those who have wronged us. We also pray in a special way for everyone who will die today. Hold them in their transition from this life to the next, and comfort their loved ones as you comforted and consoled so many people while you walked the earth.

Mary, pray for us and teach us to trust your son.

Amen.

The Glorious Mysteries

The Resurrection

Fruit of the Mystery: Faith

The Ascension

Fruit of the Mystery: Desire for Heaven

Pentecost

Fruit of the Mystery: Friendship with the Holy Spirit

The Assumption

Fruit of the Mystery: Aging and Dying Gracefully

The Crowning of Mary Queen of Heaven

Fruit of the Mystery: True Devotion to Mary

THE FIRST GLORIOUS MYSTERY

The Resurrection

Fruit of the Mystery: Faith

A Reading from the Gospel of Matthew

The Resurrection of Jesus
After the Sabbath, as the first day of the week was dawning, Mary Magdalene and the other Mary went to see the tomb. And suddenly there was a great earthquake; for an angel of the Lord, descending from heaven, came and rolled back the stone and sat on it.

His appearance was like lightning, and his clothing white as snow. For fear of him the guards shook and became like dead men. But the angel said to the women, "Do not be afraid; I know that you are looking for Jesus who was crucified. He is not here; for he has been raised, as he said. Come, see the place where he lay. Then go quickly and tell his disciples, 'He has been raised from the dead, and indeed he is going ahead of you to Galilee; there you will see him.' This is my message for you."

So they left the tomb quickly with fear and great joy, and ran to tell his disciples. Suddenly Jesus met them and said, "Greetings!" And they came to him, took hold of his feet, and worshiped him. Then Jesus said to them, "Do not be afraid; go and tell my brothers to go to Galilee; there they will see me."

Matthew 28:1–10

REFLECTION

Looking in All the Wrong Places

God does his greatest work in the midst of our greatest darkness. It is when our hearts are broken that God does some of his best work. How did the disciples feel that Friday night? Defeated and hopeless. Lost and confused. Swallowed by an all-encompassing darkness. How did they feel on Saturday? Brokenhearted perhaps. They say the darkest hour is right before the dawn, and it is in these darkest hours that God is often preparing to do his greatest work. He certainly was that Sunday morning.

Looking back on life I can see that time and time again, I was looking in the wrong places for all sorts of things. Here we find the women who loved and cared for Jesus throughout his public life looking for him in the wrong places.

The interesting thing is that Jesus had made himself clear. He had spoken using a metaphor when he said, "Destroy this temple, and in three days I will raise it up." He was telling his followers and everyone that would listen that on the third day he would rise from the dead. It was the third day—why were they so surprised? Did they not believe him? And even if they didn't understand Jesus when he first said it, here, now, in the face of the reality of the Resurrection, did they still not get it?

Whatever the case may be, it seems that since the very beginning humanity has been looking for love and happiness in all the wrong places. Are we looking for the abundant life in the wrong places today?

Now let's put ourselves there, in Jerusalem on that Sunday morning. Imagine how quickly word spread. Imagine how many versions of the story were circulating. The city would have been filled with emotion like never before: joy, anger, fear, confusion, anxiety, frustration, rage, indifference, hatred, and others.

What were the Pharisees feeling when they first heard? How did it make Pilate feel? Were the men who tortured and executed him afraid he would come back for revenge? And no doubt there were many who went on with their lives indifferently, thinking he was just another man and accepting the story that his followers had stolen his body.

It must have been some Sunday morning. The city would have been drowning in gossip and emotion. But few if any would have recognized that this was the main event of human history. Jesus rose from the dead.

On that day there were no doubt many who ignored it, and many others who doubted it, rejected it, or were skeptical or cynical. These people have existed in every age and exist today, but you see them wandering through their lives confused. It is simply impossible to make sense of life and history without acknowledging the Resurrection.

You and I are walking through the streets of Jerusalem, listening to people talk about it on that Sunday morning. Do we believe? Do we have doubts? Are we too busy attending to the urgent matters of our lives to even care?

We keep walking and decide to visit the tomb. The place is crowded, and there are guards trying to keep people away. But we stand there for a few moments quietly and wonder, What does all this mean?

Now returning to the present, what part of your life needs resurrecting today? Do you want Jesus to resurrect that part of your life? Or are you attached to the dysfunction and self-destruction?

It's time to live in the risen Lord. When we do, we are fully alive; we experience joy and ecstasy, detachment from the passing troubles of this world, and confidence that in the end truth and goodness will always prevail.

On Friday afternoon they nailed Truth and Goodness to a tree. But on Sunday morning Truth rose from the dead. You cannot kill Truth and Goodness. You can put it in a tomb, but you cannot keep it there.

PRAYER

With these inspirations in our hearts and minds, we turn to you, Jesus, and pray.

Lord, unleash the power of the Resurrection in my life today. Resurrect the area of my life that most needs it today. Help me to stop resisting your grace, stay out of your way, and let you work in me and through me in whatever ways you want.

Your Resurrection demands a response, Jesus. You have conquered death and hatred with love. Teach us to do the same in some small way in our own lives. Give us the courage to love when we are rejected, despised, hated, ignored, bullied, abused, unappreciated, and taken for granted.

Thank you, Jesus. Thank you. I pray I never let a day pass without these words crossing my lips.

Jesus, we offer this decade to you for all those who have lost faith in you, and for anyone who has never encountered you in a way that allowed them to embrace you. We beg your forgiveness for anything we have ever done that has prevented someone from knowing and loving you.

Mary, teach us to believe in your son, and to trust that he always acts with our best interests in mind.

Amen.

THE SECOND GLORIOUS MYSTERY

The Ascension

Fruit of the Mystery: Desire for Heaven

A Reading from the Acts of the Apostles

The Ascension of Jesus

So when they had come together, they asked him, "Lord, is this the time when you will restore the kingdom to Israel?" He replied, "It is not for you to know the times or periods that the Father has set by his own authority. But you will receive power when the Holy Spirit has come upon you; and you will be my witnesses in Jerusalem, in all Judea and Samaria, and to the ends of the earth."

When he had said this, as they were watching, he was lifted up, and a cloud took him out of their sight.

While he was going and they were gazing up toward heaven, suddenly two men in white robes stood by them. They said, "Men of Galilee, why do you stand looking up toward heaven? This Jesus, who has been taken up from you into heaven, will come in the same way as you saw him go into heaven."

Acts 1:6–11

REFLECTION

Jesus' Enemies

There are two sides to every story. When they dragged Jesus before Pilate, they thought that would be it. When they watched him being scourged, they thought no man could endure and survive it, but he did. When they crowned him with thorns, they mocked him, thinking there could be no retribution.

When he was sent out to Golgotha to carry a cross, they celebrated that their will was being done. When they nailed him to the cross, they thought they were rid of him forever. When he mumbled from the cross, they thought he was a madman. And when he screamed out in the agony a man feels when death is near, they thought they had won.

But what they thought was the end was only the beginning.

When the tomb was empty, they claimed it was fraud. When they learned the truth, they were afraid. When he started appearing to people, their illusion crumbled. When his followers rose up and peacefully told his story wherever people would listen, their fear grew.

When they harassed his followers, they were met with peace, and they were perplexed. When they watched his communities living around love, respect, kindness, compassion, and generosity, they were baffled. And when in the face of death his followers showed hope, not fear, they were intrigued and amazed.

There are two sides to every story. What side of the story are you going to place yourself?

What does it mean to ascend? It means to rise. Christians are called and challenged every day to ascend above situations. The opposite of ascend is descend. The world encourages us to descend into the-worst-version-of-ourselves. But every day we are called to ascend and become the-very-best-version-of-ourselves.

Now, place yourself there with the disciples as Jesus bids them farewell and sends them out to change the world. After forty days of eating and drinking with his disciples, Jesus ascends body and soul into heaven.

Jesus did exactly what he said he would do. He was a man of his word. Why do we ignore and doubt his words so often?

He said he would return one day. Do you ever think about it? Imagine if he came today. Are you ready? Would we recognize him? God's chosen people missed him the first time. Would we miss him the second time?

PRAYER

With these inspirations in our hearts and minds, we turn to you, Jesus, and pray.

Lord, give us the courage to take you at your word, and to take your words seriously. Help us to resist the temptation to water down your words or pretend that they are anything but an invitation to radically change our lives.

Jesus, teach us to ascend beyond mediocrity, laziness, self-deception, procrastination, fear, doubt, instant gratification, self-sabotage, indecision, escapism, self-loathing, pride, and selfishness.

We resolve today, Lord, to listen more carefully to the words of the Gospel, and to try harder than ever before to live them in our lives.

Jesus, we offer this decade to you for our homeland and the people of that land. Bless our homeland with faith and values that help everyone in society to ascend. We also pray in a special way for anyone who is living in a country other than the country of their birth, especially those who have been forced to relocate against their will. Liberate all men and women, in all countries, from prejudice against the immigrant and stranger. Remind us that we are all immigrants on this earth, just passing through, pilgrims on our way to our true home with you in heaven.

Mary, please pray that we can let go of any petty prejudices that we allow to rule our hearts, minds, and lives.

Amen.

THE THIRD GLORIOUS MYSTERY

Pentecost

Fruit of the Mystery: Friendship with the Holy Spirit

A Reading from the Acts of the Apostles

The Coming of the Holy Spirit

When the day of Pentecost had come, they were all together in one place. And suddenly from heaven there came a sound like the rush of a violent wind, and it filled the entire house where they were sitting. Divided tongues, as of fire, appeared among them, and a tongue rested on each of them. All of them were filled with the Holy Spirit and began to speak in other languages, as the Spirit gave them ability.

Now there were devout Jews from every nation under heaven living in Jerusalem. And at this sound the crowd gathered and was bewildered, because each one heard them speaking in the native language of each. Amazed and astonished, they asked, "Are not all these who are speaking Galileans? And how is it that we hear, each of us, in our own native language?"

Acts 2:1–8

REFLECTION

What Are You Afraid Of?

The disciples were afraid. Most of us have probably never experienced fear like the fear that gripped them. They were afraid for their lives—afraid the mob would kill them, yes, but also afraid of what was next for them. What would they do now that Jesus was gone?

Then the Holy Spirit descended upon them and transformed them. Their fear was banished, and they were filled with courage. This is the greatest before-and-after sequence the world has ever seen.

Imagine yourself there, in the Upper Room. There is an eerie silence. The fear is palpable. Then the wind begins to blow and the shutters on the windows rattle, and the wind keeps growing until it is howling, and now the shutters are shaking so violently that you sense at any moment they will be ripped from their hinges and fly off into the night. But then an incredible peace descends upon the room and fills the disciples, reminding them of the peace they felt the first day they agreed to follow Jesus. You feel this deep peace too, and you want to hold on to it so it never ends. But then the disciples begin to stir; they get up, filled with a new sense of urgency. The contrast is blinding. A few minutes ago they were paralyzed by fear; now they are animated with a boldness and courage you have never seen before. They begin to leave the Upper Room, and you are left sitting there. Should you go with them? Should you stay put? Should you go back to your ordinary life and pretend you never experienced what you just experienced?

We all need what I like to call a Pentecost Moment, that moment when things finally click into place and the genius of Catholicism makes sense to us. For some people it is a book; for others it is a retreat such as Welcome, or a pilgrimage. There are millions of baptized Catholics and non-Catholic Christians who have not yet experienced their Pentecost Moment. You and I are called and chosen to collaborate with God and help facilitate them.

But our transformation doesn't occur in a single moment. That is just the beginning, the jolt that gets us to see that we are sleepwalking through life and awakens us to all the possibilities.

Now we need daily conversion to chase the selfishness from our hearts, minds, bodies, and souls. But we resist this ongoing transformation into the-very-best-version-of-ourselves. We resist the very things that will make us happy. This is the great paradox of our lives.

Why won't we surrender once and for all to God and allow him to do powerful things in us and through us? What are we afraid of?

PRAYER

With these inspirations in our hearts and minds, we turn to you, Jesus, and pray.

Jesus, send the Holy Spirit upon us again today. Liberate us from our fears and give us the courage to make ourselves 100 percent available to you.

Raise up more ministries and disciples dedicated to creating Pentecost Moments for men, women, and children who have never had a chance to really know your dreams for their lives. Remove from us the false contentment that makes us comfortable with maintenance and mediocrity. Give us a hunger for mission. Open our eyes to see all the people around us who are drowning spiritually, and give us the courage to throw them a lifeline.

Jesus, we offer this decade of the Rosary as a prayer begging you to unleash a new Pentecost in the lives of millions of people. We pray for anyone who will encounter a Pentecost Moment today. Give them a vision of how much better their lives will be if they follow you, and give them the courage to embrace this opportunity. We also ask you to renew our commitment to mission. Finally, we pray in a very special way for anyone who has had his or her image of God corrupted. Heal them so they can discover your love and providence like never before.

Mary, please pray for us that we will learn to hear God's voice in our lives more clearly with every passing day, and teach us to become great friends with the Holy Spirit.

Amen.

THE FOURTH GLORIOUS MYSTERY

The Assumption

Fruit of the Mystery: Aging and Dying Gracefully

A Reading from the Book of Revelation

A Woman Clothed with the Sun
Then God's temple in heaven was opened, and within his temple was seen the ark of his covenant. And there came flashes of lightning, rumblings, peals of thunder, an earthquake and a great hailstorm.

A great and wondrous sign appeared in heaven: a woman clothed with the sun, with the moon under her feet and a crown of twelve stars on her head. She was pregnant and cried out in pain as she was about to give birth.

Then another sign appeared in heaven: an enormous red dragon with seven heads and ten horns and seven crowns on his heads.... The dragon stood in front of the woman who was about to give birth, so that he might devour her child the moment it was born. She gave birth to a son, a male child, who will rule all the nations with an iron scepter.

Revelation 11:19, 12:1–5

REFLECTION

The Next Life
There is another reality we know almost nothing about. What is heaven like? People have been speculating for thousands of years, yet in truth nobody knows. But it is good for us from

time to time to think about what it might be like, and at the same time to be ever mindful that it is infinitely better than we can even imagine. St. Paul reminds us, "No eye has seen, no ear has heard, and no heart can conceive, what God has prepared for those who love him" (1 Corinthians 2:9). Heaven is more beautiful than the most beautiful thing you have ever seen. It is more beautiful than the most beautiful thing you have ever heard. We are simply incapable of conceiving how amazing heaven is.

One of the greatest spiritual dangers is intellectual pride. It is so easy to fall into the trap of thinking we know a lot, when in reality even those among us who know the most know very little. What we don't know about God dwarfs what we do know about God. And when it comes to the afterlife, we know even less.

Pride, arrogance, and ego can all play large roles in our lives and become huge obstacles that prevent us from hearing God's voice clearly. But in Mary we find the antidote for all three: humility.

Mary's radical humility is an encyclopedia of lessons about the inner life. Imagine how rich her inner life must have been. Imagine what it was like for the first Christians to seek her counsel and guidance. Then, at the end of her life, Mary was taken body and soul into heaven, her reward for a life lived entirely for God.

What's keeping you from just giving everything to God? It's hard to do when you are still in love with your sins, when you are obsessed with what other people think about you, when you like to be the one in control. Are you ready to surrender once and for all to God? How would your life be different if you did?

PRAYER

With these inspirations in our hearts and minds, we turn to you, Jesus, and pray.

Lord, fill us with a desire for heaven. Help us to want to be with you more than anything this world has to offer. And give us the grace and courage to strive for heroic virtue, become the-best-version-of-ourselves, and live holy lives.

Jesus, we offer this decade to you for all those people who have never had the joy and privilege of knowing you and your mother. We pray in a special way for the men and women of other religions; inspire them to rigorously seek truth and never be afraid of where it might lead them.

Mary, remind us that we are pilgrims passing through this world, and teach us to age and die gracefully.

Amen.

THE FIFTH GLORIOUS MYSTERY

The Crowning of Mary Queen of Heaven

Fruit of the Mystery: True Devotion to Mary

A Reading from the First Letter of Peter

The Crown of Glory that Never Fades

Now as an elder myself and a witness of the sufferings of Christ, as well as one who shares in the glory to be revealed, I exhort the elders among you to tend the flock of God that is in your charge, exercising the oversight, not under compulsion but willingly, as God would have you do it—not for sordid gain but eagerly. Do not lord it over those in your charge, but be examples to the flock. And when the chief shepherd appears, you will win the crown of glory that never fades away. In the same way, you who are younger must accept the authority of the elders. And all of you must clothe yourselves with humility in your dealings with one another, for "God opposes the proud, but gives grace to the humble."

Humble yourselves therefore under the mighty hand of God, so that he may exalt you in due time. Cast all your anxiety on him, because he cares for you. Discipline yourselves, keep alert. Like a roaring lion your adversary the devil prowls around, looking for someone to devour. Resist him, steadfast in your faith, for you know that your brothers and sisters in all the world are undergoing the same kinds of suffering. And after you have suffered for a little while, the God of all grace, who has called you to his eternal glory in Christ, will himself restore, support, strengthen, and establish you. To him be the power forever and ever. Amen.

1 Peter 5:1–11

REFLECTION

Context Is Beautiful

The glory of this world fades, and fades quickly. And yet so often we chase the glory of this fleeting world with reckless abandon. Many men and women will do anything to accomplish glory in this world.

Jesus invites us to seek eternal glory with the same energy and zeal. Are you more passionate and enthusiastic about the things of this world or the things of the next world? Are you more passionate about accumulating things in this world than about caring for the less fortunate, relieving the suffering of the poor, and working to eradicate injustice?

God invites us to look at everything in the context of eternity. Context is a beautiful thing, because it shows us the true value of things. A billionaire cares little about his money if his five-year-old son has cancer. That's context. When the doctor tells you that you have only six months to live, you very quickly develop clarity around what matters most and what matters least. That's context.

Context gives us the clarity we need to make great decisions.

The presence of Jesus in her life allowed Mary to constantly see things in the context of love and eternity. If we ask her to accompany us in our journey, she will share this perspective with us, and we will discover the true value of things.

Unless we allow love to rearrange our priorities, when death comes to us, as it comes to us all eventually, our hearts will be filled with regret . . . and that is a horrible way to die.

Mary, your courage, fidelity, and humility greatly pleased the Father, Son, and the Holy Spirit, and now they crown you Queen of Heaven. Mother of God, no greater title exists on earth, as no greater creature than you existed. Queen of Heaven: Other than God, no greater title exists in heaven.

This Mary, who is your spiritual mother and mine, is the most celebrated woman on earth and in heaven. Who is greater than Mary? None but God.

PRAYER

With these inspirations in our hearts and minds, we turn to you, Jesus, and pray.

Lord, open the eyes of my soul a little more each day so I can see things as they really are. Rearrange my priorities around love of God and love of neighbor. Put everything in my life in the context of gospel values and eternity so I can see the true value of things.

Jesus, I offer you this decade in gratitude for this day and all the blessings you have filled my life with. Forgive me for the times I have dwelled in my selfishness and been ungrateful. I am especially grateful for the gift of faith and the grace to pray this Rosary today. Who knows where I would be and what I would be doing without your gentle and persistent call to live a life of virtue?

Mary, thank you for this opportunity to pray with you. Wrap me in your mantle, wrap my family and friends in your mantle, wrap all of humanity in the protection of your mantle.

Amen.

PART
THREE

9

A Scriptural Rosary

A Scriptural Rosary is quite simple. It consists of individual verses from the Bible. One Bible verse is read before each Hail Mary, and each verse builds upon the preceding, unveiling the story behind the mystery that you are pondering.

God speaks to us through the Bible. In the Scriptural Rosary, he teaches us about the most important moments of Jesus' life. Watching these incredible happenings unfold one verse at a time can be very inspiring.

Whether you're new to the Rosary or have been praying it your whole life, you may find the variety of the Scriptural Rosary invigorating. Some people do, and some people don't, and that's OK. Everything doesn't have to be for everyone.

The Joyful Mysteries

The Annunciation

Our Father...

1. In the sixth month the angel Gabriel was sent by God to a town in Galilee called Nazareth, to a virgin engaged to a man whose name was Joseph, of the house of David. (*Luke 1:26–27*)

Hail Mary...

2. The virgin's name was Mary. (*Luke 1:27*)

Hail Mary...

3. The angel Gabriel came to Mary and said, "Greetings, favored one! The Lord is with you!" (*Luke 1:28*)

Hail Mary...

4. But Mary was much perplexed by his words and pondered what sort of greeting this might be. (*Luke 1:29*)

Hail Mary...

5. The angel said to her, "Do not be afraid, Mary, for you have found favor with God. (*Luke 1:30*)

Hail Mary...

6. "And now, you will conceive in your womb and bear a son, and you will name him Jesus." (*Luke 1:31*)

Hail Mary...

7. Mary said to the angel, "How can this be, since I am a virgin?" *(Luke 1:34)*

Hail Mary . . .

8. The angel said to her, "The Holy Spirit will come upon you, and the power of the Most High will overshadow you; therefore the child to be born will be holy; he will be called Son of God. *(Luke 1:35)*

Hail Mary . . .

9. Then Mary said, "Here am I, the servant of the Lord; let it be with me according to your word." *(Luke 1:38)*

Hail Mary . . .

10. The Word became flesh and lived among us, and we have seen his glory, the glory as of a father's only son, full of grace and truth. *(John 1:14)*

Hail Mary . . .
Glory Be . . .

The Visitation

Our Father ...

1. In those days Mary set out and went with haste to a Judean town in the hill country, where she entered the house of Zechariah and greeted Elizabeth. *(Luke 1:39–40)*

    Hail Mary ...

2. When Elizabeth heard Mary's greeting, the child leaped in her womb. *(Luke 1:41)*

    Hail Mary ...

3. Elizabeth was filled with the Holy Spirit. *(Luke 1:41)*

    Hail Mary ...

4. She exclaimed with a loud cry, "Blessed are you among women, and blessed is the fruit of your womb." *(Luke 1:42)*

    Hail Mary ...

5. "Why has this happened to me, that the mother of my Lord comes to me?" *(Luke 1:43)*

    Hail Mary ...

6. Mary said, "My soul magnifies the Lord." *(Luke 1:46)*

    Hail Mary ...

7. "My spirit rejoices in God my Savior." *(Luke 1:47)*

Hail Mary . . .

8. "He has looked with favor on the lowliness of his servant." *(Luke 1:48)*

Hail Mary . . .

9. "Surely, from now on all generations will call me blessed." *(Luke 1:48)*

Hail Mary . . .

10. "The Mighty One has done great things for me, and holy is his name." *(Luke 1:49)*

Hail Mary . . .
Glory Be . . .

The Birth of Jesus

Our Father...

1. While Mary and Joseph were in Bethlehem, the time came for her to deliver her child. *(Luke 2:6)*

   Hail Mary...

2. She gave birth to her firstborn son and wrapped him in bands of cloth, and laid him in a manger, because there was no place for them in the inn. *(Luke 2:7)*

   Hail Mary...

3. In that region there were shepherds out in the field, keeping watch over their flock by night. *(Luke 2:8)*

   Hail Mary...

4. Then an angel of the Lord stood before them, and the glory of the Lord shone around them, and they were terrified. *(Luke 2:9)*

   Hail Mary...

5. The angel said to them, "Do not be afraid; for see—I am bringing you good news of great joy for all the people." *(Luke 2:10)*

   Hail Mary...

6. To you is born this day in the city of David a Savior, who is the Messiah, the Lord." *(Luke 2:11)*

Hail Mary . . .

7. Suddenly there was with the angel a multitude of the heavenly host, praising God and saying, "Glory to God in the highest heaven, and on earth peace among those whom he favors!" *(Luke 2:13–14)*

Hail Mary . . .

8. In the time of King Herod, after Jesus was born in Bethlehem of Judea, wise men from the East came to Jerusalem. *(Matthew 2:1)*

Hail Mary . . .

9. On entering the house, they saw the child with Mary his mother; and they knelt down and paid him homage. *(Matthew 2:11)*

Hail Mary . . .

10. Then, opening their treasure chests, they offered him gifts of gold, frankincense, and myrrh. *(Matthew 2:11)*

Hail Mary . . .
Glory Be . . .

The Presentation

Our Father . . .

1. When the time came for their purification according to the law of Moses, Mary and Joseph brought the child Jesus up to Jerusalem to present him to the Lord. *(Luke 2:22)*

Hail Mary . . .

2. Now there was a man in Jerusalem whose name was Simeon; this man was righteous and devout, looking forward to the consolation of Israel, and the Holy Spirit rested on him. *(Luke 2:25)*

Hail Mary . . .

3. It had been revealed to him by the Holy Spirit that he would not see death before he had seen the Lord's Messiah. *(Luke 2:26)*

Hail Mary . . .

4. Guided by the Spirit, Simeon came into the temple; and the parents brought in the child Jesus. *(Luke 2:27)*

Hail Mary . . .

5. Simeon took him in his arms and praised God, saying, "Master, now you are dismissing your servant in peace, according to your word." *(Luke 2:28–29)*

Hail Mary . . .

6. "My eyes have seen your salvation, which you have prepared in the presence of all peoples." *(Luke 2:30–31)*

Hail Mary . . .

7. "A light for revelation to the Gentiles and for glory to your people Israel." *(Luke 2:32)*

Hail Mary . . .

8. Simeon blessed them and said to his mother Mary, "This child is destined for the falling and the rising of many in Israel, and to be a sign that will be opposed." *(Luke 2:34)*

Hail Mary . . .

9. "The inner thoughts of many will be revealed—and a sword will pierce your own soul too." *(Luke 2:35)*

Hail Mary . . .

10. The child grew and became strong, filled with wisdom; and the favor of God was upon him. *(Luke 2:40)*

Hail Mary . . .
Glory Be . . .

Finding the Child Jesus in the Temple

Our Father...

1. Now every year Jesus' parents went to Jerusalem for the festival of the Passover. And when he was twelve years old, they went up as usual for the festival. *(Luke 2:41–42)*

Hail Mary...

2. When the festival was ended and they started to return, the boy Jesus stayed behind in Jerusalem, but his parents did not know it. *(Luke 2:43)*

Hail Mary...

3. When they did not find him, they returned to Jerusalem to search for him. *(Luke 2:45)*

Hail Mary...

4. After three days they found him in the temple, sitting among the teachers, listening to them and asking them questions. *(Luke 2:46)*

Hail Mary...

5. All who heard him were amazed at his understanding and his answers. *(Luke 2:47)*

Hail Mary...

6. When his parents saw him they were astonished; and his mother said to him, "Child, why have you treated us like this? Look, your father and I have been searching for you in great anxiety." *(Luke 2:48)*

Hail Mary . . .

7. Jesus said to them, "Why were you searching for me? Did you not know that I must be in my Father's house?" *(Luke 2:49)*

Hail Mary . . .

8. They did not understand what he said to them. *(Luke 2:50)*

Hail Mary . . .

9. Then he went down with them and came to Nazareth, and was obedient to them. *(Luke 2:51)*

Hail Mary . . .

10. His mother treasured all these things in her heart. *(Luke 2:51)*

Hail Mary . . .
Glory Be . . .

The Luminous Mysteries

The Baptism of Jesus in the River Jordan

Our Father ...

1. John the Baptist said, "I am the voice of one crying out in the wilderness, 'Make straight the way of the Lord,' as the prophet Isaiah said." *(John 1:23)*

    Hail Mary ...

2. "The one who is more powerful than I is coming after me; I am not worthy to stoop down and untie the thong of his sandals." *(Mark 1:7)*

    Hail Mary ...

3. "I baptize you with water for repentance, but one who is more powerful than I is coming after me; he will baptize you with the Holy Spirit and fire." *(Matthew 3:11)*

    Hail Mary ...

4. Then Jesus came from Galilee to John at the Jordan, to be baptized by him. *(Matthew 3:13)*

    Hail Mary ...

5. John saw Jesus coming toward him and declared, "Here is the Lamb of God who takes away the sin of the world!" *(John 1:29)*

    Hail Mary ...

6. John would have prevented him, saying, "I need to be baptized by you, and do you come to me?" *(Matthew 3:14)*

Hail Mary . . .

7. Jesus answered him, "Let it be so now; for it is proper for us in this way to fulfill all righteousness." Then John consented. *(Matthew 3:15)*

Hail Mary . . .

8. When Jesus had been baptized, just as he came up from the water, suddenly the heavens were opened to him and he saw the Spirit of God descending like a dove and alighting on him. *(Matthew 3:16)*

Hail Mary . . .

9. A voice from heaven said, "This is my Son, the Beloved, with whom I am well pleased." *(Matthew 3:17)*

Hail Mary . . .

10. The Spirit immediately drove him out into the wilderness where he was tempted by Satan. *(Mark 1:12–13)*

Hail Mary . . .
Glory Be . . .

The Wedding Feast at Cana

Our Father . . .

1. There was a marriage in Cana of Galilee, and the mother of Jesus was there. *(John 2:1)*

   Hail Mary . . .

2. When the wine gave out, the mother of Jesus said to him, "They have no wine." *(John 2:3)*

   Hail Mary . . .

3. Jesus said to her, "Woman, what concern is that to you and to me? My hour has not yet come." *(John 2:4)*

   Hail Mary . . .

4. His mother said to the servants, "Do whatever he tells you." *(John 2:5)*

   Hail Mary . . .

5. Now standing there were six stone water jars for the Jewish rites of purification, each holding twenty or thirty gallons. *(John 2:6)*

   Hail Mary . . .

6. Jesus said to the servants, "Fill the jars with water." And they filled them up to the brim. *(John 2:7)*

Hail Mary . . .

7. He said to the servants, "Now draw some out, and take it to the chief steward." So they took it. *(John 2:8)*

Hail Mary . . .

8. When the steward tasted the water that had become wine, and did not know where it came from, the steward called the bridegroom. *(John 2:9)*

Hail Mary . . .

9. The steward said to him, "Everyone serves the good wine first, and then the inferior wine after the guests have become drunk. But you have kept the good wine until now." *(John 2:10)*

Hail Mary . . .

10. Jesus did this, the first of his signs, in Cana of Galilee, and revealed his glory; and his disciples believed in him. *(John 2:11)*

Hail Mary . . .
Glory Be . . .

The Proclamation of the Kingdom of God

Our Father...

1. Jesus came to Galilee, proclaiming the good news of God, and saying, "The time is fulfilled, and the kingdom of God has come near; repent, and believe in the good news." *(Mark 1:14–15)*

Hail Mary...

2. "Very truly, I tell you, no one can enter the kingdom of God without being born of water and Spirit." *(John 3:5)*

Hail Mary...

3. "Blessed are the poor in spirit, for theirs is the kingdom of heaven." *(Matthew 5:3)*

Hail Mary...

4. "Blessed are those who are persecuted for righteousness' sake, for theirs is the kingdom of heaven." *(Matthew 5:10)*

Hail Mary...

5. "I tell you, unless your righteousness exceeds that of the scribes and Pharisees, you will never enter the kingdom of heaven." *(Matthew 5:20)*

Hail Mary...

6. "The kingdom of heaven is like a merchant in search of fine pearls; on finding one pearl of great value, went and sold all that he had and bought it." *(Matthew 13:45–46)*

Hail Mary . . .

7. "Truly I tell you, unless you change and become like children, you will never enter the kingdom of heaven." *(Matthew 18:3)*

Hail Mary . . .

8. The disciples were perplexed at these words. But Jesus said to them again, "Children, how hard it is to enter the kingdom of God!" *(Mark 10:24)*

Hail Mary . . .

9. "I must proclaim the good news of the kingdom of God to the other cities also; for I was sent for this purpose." *(Luke 4:43)*

Hail Mary . . .

10. "You are those who have stood by me in my trials; and I confer on you, just as my Father has conferred on me, a kingdom, so that you may eat and drink at my table in my kingdom." *(Luke 22:28–30)*

Hail Mary . . .
Glory Be . . .

The Transfiguration of Jesus

Our Father . . .

1. Now about eight days after these sayings Jesus took with him Peter and John and James, and went up on the mountain to pray. *(Luke 9:28)*

   Hail Mary . . .

2. Jesus was transfigured before them, and his face shone like the sun, and his clothes became dazzling white. *(Matthew 17:2)*

   Hail Mary . . .

3. Suddenly there appeared Moses and Elijah, talking with Jesus. *(Matthew 17:3)*

   Hail Mary . . .

4. They appeared in glory and were speaking of Jesus' departure, which he was about to accomplish at Jerusalem. *(Luke 9:31)*

   Hail Mary . . .

5. Then Peter said to Jesus, "Lord, it is good for us to be here; if you wish, I will make three dwellings here, one for you, one for Moses, and one for Elijah." *(Matthew 17:4)*

   Hail Mary . . .

6. While he was saying this, a cloud came and overshadowed Peter, John, and James; and they were terrified as they entered the cloud. *(Luke 9:34)*

Hail Mary . . .

7. Then from the cloud came a voice that said, "This is my Son, my Chosen; listen to him!" *(Luke 9:35)*

Hail Mary . . .

8. Suddenly when they looked around, they saw no one with them any more, but only Jesus. *(Mark 9:8)*

Hail Mary . . .

9. As they were coming down the mountain, he ordered them to tell no one about what they had seen, until after the Son of Man had risen from the dead. *(Mark 9:9)*

Hail Mary . . .

10. So they kept the matter to themselves, questioning what this rising from the dead could mean. *(Mark 9:10)*

Hail Mary . . .
Glory Be . . .

The Institution of the Eucharist

Our Father . . .

1. On the first day of Unleavened Bread, when the Passover lamb is sacrificed, his disciples said to Jesus, "Where do you want us to go and make the preparations for you to eat the Passover?" *(Mark 14:12)*

Hail Mary . . .

2. He said, "Go into the city to a certain man, and say to him, 'The Teacher says, My time is near; I will keep the Passover at your house with my disciples.'" *(Matthew 26:18)*

Hail Mary . . .

3. When the hour came, Jesus took his place at the table, and the apostles with him. *(Luke 22:14)*

Hail Mary . . .

4. He said to them, "I have eagerly desired to eat this Passover with you before I suffer." *(Luke 22:15)*

Hail Mary . . .

5. The Lord Jesus took a loaf of bread, and when he had given thanks, he broke it and said, "This is my body that is for you. Do this in remembrance of me." *(1 Corinthians 11:23–24)*

Hail Mary . . .

6. In the same way he took the cup also, after supper, saying, "This cup is the new covenant in my blood. Do this, as often as you drink it, in remembrance of me." *(1 Corinthians 11:25)*

Hail Mary . . .

7. For as often as you eat this bread and drink the cup, you proclaim the Lord's death until he comes. *(1 Corinthians 11:26)*

Hail Mary . . .

8. The cup of blessing that we bless, is it not a sharing in the blood of Christ? *(1 Corinthians 10:16)*

Hail Mary . . .

9. The bread that we break, is it not a sharing in the body of Christ? *(1 Corinthians 10:16)*

Hail Mary . . .

10. Because there is one bread, we who are many are one body, for we all partake of the one bread. *(1 Corinthians 10:17)*

Hail Mary . . .
Glory Be . . .

The Sorrowful Mysteries

The Agony in the Garden

Our Father ...

1. Then Jesus went with them to a place called Gethsemane; and he said to his disciples, "Sit here while I go over there and pray." *(Matthew 26:36)*

   Hail Mary ...

2. He took with him Peter and the two sons of Zebedee, and began to be grieved and agitated. *(Matthew 26:37)*

   Hail Mary ...

3. Then he said to them, "I am deeply grieved, even to death; remain here, and stay awake with me." *(Matthew 26:38)*

   Hail Mary ...

4. He withdrew from them about a stone's throw, and knelt down and prayed, "Father, if you are willing, remove this chalice from me; nevertheless not my will, but yours, be done." *(Luke 22:41–42)*

   Hail Mary ...

5. Then an angel from heaven appeared to him and gave him strength. *(Luke 22:43)*

   Hail Mary ...

6. In his anguish he prayed more earnestly, and his sweat became like great drops of blood falling down on the ground. *(Luke 22:44)*

Hail Mary...

7. Then he came to the disciples and found them sleeping; and he said to Peter, "So, could you not stay awake with me one hour?" *(Matthew 26:40)*

Hail Mary...

8. "Stay awake and pray that you may not come into the time of trial; the spirit indeed is willing, but the flesh is weak." *(Matthew 26:41)*

Hail Mary...

9. While he was still speaking, suddenly a crowd came, and the one called Judas, one of the twelve, was leading them. *(Luke 22:47)*

Hail Mary...

10. He approached Jesus to kiss him; but Jesus said to him, "Judas, is it with a kiss that you are betraying the Son of Man?" *(Luke 22:47–48)*

Hail Mary...
Glory Be...

The Scourging at the Pillar

Our Father...

1. As soon as it was morning, the chief priests bound Jesus, led him away, and handed him over to Pilate, who asked him, "Are you the King of the Jews?" *(Mark 15:1–2)*

Hail Mary...

2. Jesus answered, "My kingdom is not from this world. If my kingdom were from this world, my followers would be fighting to keep me from being handed over to the Jews. But as it is, my kingdom is not from here." *(John 18:36)*

Hail Mary...

3. "For this I was born, and for this I came into the world, to testify to the truth. Everyone who belongs to the truth listens to my voice." *(John 18:37)*

Hail Mary...

4. Pilate asked him, "What is truth?" *(John 18:38)*

Hail Mary...

5. After he had said this, he went out to the Jews again and told them, "I find no case against him; I will therefore have him flogged and release him."*(John 18:38; Luke 23:16)*

Hail Mary...

6. Then they all shouted out together, "Away with this fellow!" So Pilate took Jesus and had him flogged. *(Luke 23:18; John 19:1)*

Hail Mary . . .

7. He was despised and rejected by others; a man of suffering and acquainted with infirmity; and as one from whom others hide their faces he was despised, and we held him of no account. *(Isaiah 53:3)*

Hail Mary . . .

8. He was oppressed, and he was afflicted, yet he did not open his mouth; like a lamb that is led to the slaughter, and like a sheep that before its shearers is silent, so he did not open his mouth. *(Isaiah 53:7)*

Hail Mary . . .

9. Surely he has borne our infirmities and carried our diseases; yet we accounted him stricken, struck down by God, and afflicted. *(Isaiah 53:4)*

Hail Mary . . .

10. But he was wounded for our transgressions, crushed for our iniquities; upon him was the punishment that made us whole, and by his bruises we are healed. *(Isaiah 53:5)*

Hail Mary . . .
Glory Be . . .

The Crowning with Thorns

Our Father . . .

1. Then the soldiers of the governor took Jesus into the governor's headquarters, and they gathered the whole cohort around him. *(Matthew 27:27)*

Hail Mary . . .

2. They stripped him and put a scarlet robe on him. *(Matthew 27:28)*

Hail Mary . . .

3. After twisting some thorns into a crown, they put it on his head. *(Matthew 27:29)*

Hail Mary . . .

4. They put a reed in his right hand and knelt before him and mocked him, saying, "Hail, King of the Jews!" *(Matthew 27:29)*

Hail Mary . . .

5. They spat on him, and took the reed and stuck him on the head. *(Matthew 27:30)*

Hail Mary . . .

6. They kept coming up to him saying, "Hail, King of the Jews!" and striking him on the face. *(John 19:3)*

Hail Mary...

7. Pilate went out again and said to them, "Look, I am bringing him out to you to let you know that I find no case against him." *(John 19:4)*

Hail Mary...

8. So Jesus came out, wearing the crown of thorns and the purple robe. *(John 19:5)*

Hail Mary...

9. Pilate asked them, "Shall I crucify your King?" *(John 19:15)*

Hail Mary...

10. The chief priests answered, "We have no king but the emperor." *(John 19:15)*

Hail Mary...
Glory Be...

The Carrying of the Cross

Our Father . . .

1. The chief priests took Jesus; and carrying the cross by himself, he went out to what is called The Place of the Skull, which in Hebrew is called Golgotha. *(John 19:16–17)*

Hail Mary . . .

2. As they led him away, they seized a man, Simon of Cyrene, who was coming from the country. *(Luke 23:26)*

Hail Mary . . .

3. They laid the cross on Simon, and made him carry it behind Jesus. *(Luke 23:26)*

Hail Mary . . .

4. A great number of the people followed him, and among them were women who were beating their breasts and wailing for him. *(Luke 23:27)*

Hail Mary . . .

5. Jesus turned to them and said, "Daughters of Jerusalem, do not weep for me, but weep for yourselves and for your children." *(Luke 23:28)*

Hail Mary . . .

6. Two others also, who were criminals, were led away to be put to death with him. *(Luke 23:32)*

Hail Mary ...

7. Jesus said to them all, "If any want to become my followers, let them deny themselves and take up their cross daily and follow me." *(Luke 9:23)*

Hail Mary ...

8. "Come to me, all you that are weary and are carrying heavy burdens, and I will give you rest." *(Matthew 11:28)*

Hail Mary ...

9. "Take my yoke upon you, and learn from me; for I am gentle and humble in heart, and you will find rest for your souls." *(Matthew 11:29)*

Hail Mary ...

10. "For my yoke is easy, and my burden is light." *(Matthew 11:30)*

Hail Mary ...
Glory Be ...

The Crucifixion of Jesus

Our Father...

1. When they came to the place that is called The Skull, they crucified Jesus there with the criminals, one on his right and one on his left. *(Luke 23:33)*

Hail Mary...

2. Then Jesus said, "Father, forgive them; for they do not know what they are doing." *(Luke 23:34)*

Hail Mary...

3. One of the criminals who were hanged there said, "Jesus, remember me when you come into your kingdom." *(Luke 23:39, 42)*

Hail Mary...

4. Jesus replied, "Truly I tell you, today you will be with me in Paradise." *(Luke 23:43)*

Hail Mary...

5. Meanwhile, standing near the cross of Jesus were his mother and the disciple whom he loved. *(John 19:25–26)*

Hail Mary...

6. Jesus said to his mother, "Woman, here is your son." Then he said to the disciple, "Here is your mother." *(John 19:26–27)*

> *Hail Mary . . .*

7. It was now about noon, and darkness came over the whole land until three in the afternoon. *(Luke 23:44)*

> *Hail Mary . . .*

8. Then he bowed his head and gave up his spirit. *(John 19:30)*

> *Hail Mary . . .*

9. Then Jesus, crying with a loud voice, said, "Father, into your hands I commend my spirit." *(Luke 23:46)*

> *Hail Mary . . .*

10. At that moment the curtain of the temple was torn in two, from top to bottom. The earth shook, and the rocks were split. *(Matthew 27:51)*

> *Hail Mary . . .*
> *Glory Be . . .*

The Glorious Mysteries

The Resurrection

Our Father . . .

1. "Very truly, I tell you, you will weep and mourn, but the world will rejoice; you will have pain, but your pain will turn into joy." *(John 16:20)*

Hail Mary . . .

2. "You have pain now; but I will see you again, and your hearts will rejoice, and no one will take your joy from you." *(John 16:22)*

Hail Mary . . .

3. On the first day of the week, at early dawn, the women who had come with him from Galilee came to the tomb, taking the spices that they had prepared. *(Luke 24:1)*

Hail Mary . . .

4. Suddenly there was a great earthquake; for an angel of the Lord, descending from heaven, came and rolled back the stone and sat on it. *(Matthew 28:2)*

Hail Mary . . .

5. The angel said to the women, "Do not be afraid; I know that you are looking for Jesus who was crucified. He is not here." *(Matthew 28:5–6)*

Hail Mary . . .

6. "Jesus has been raised, as he said. Come, see the place where he lay." *(Matthew 28:6)*

Hail Mary...

7. "Then go quickly and tell his disciples, 'He has been raised from the dead.'" *(Matthew 28:7)*

Hail Mary...

8. So they left the tomb quickly with fear and great joy, and ran to tell his disciples. *(Matthew 28:8)*

Hail Mary...

9. Later Jesus appeared to the eleven themselves as they were sitting at the table. *(Mark 16:14)*

Hail Mary...

10. Now on that same day two of them were going to a village called Emmaus, about seven miles from Jerusalem, and talking with each other about all these things that had happened. While they were walking and discussing, Jesus himself came near and went with them, but their eyes were kept from recognizing him. *(Luke 24:13–16)*

Hail Mary...
Glory Be...

The Ascension

Our Father ...

1. When he had said this, as they were watching, he was lifted up, and a cloud took him out of their sight. *(Acts 1:9)*

Hail Mary ...

2. The Lord Jesus was taken up into heaven and sat down at the right hand of God. *(Mark 16:19)*

Hail Mary ...

3. God highly exalted him and gave him the name that is above every name. *(Philippians 2:9)*

Hail Mary ...

4. Without any doubt, the mystery of our religion is great: He was revealed in flesh, vindicated in spirit, seen by angels, proclaimed among Gentiles, believed in throughout the world, taken up in glory. *(1 Timothy 3:16)*

Hail Mary ...

5. Through him you have come to trust in God, who raised him from the dead and gave him glory, so that your faith and hope are set on God. *(1 Peter 1:21)*

Hail Mary ...

6. Therefore it is said, "When he ascended on high he made captivity itself a captive; he gave gifts to his people." *(Ephesians 4:8)*

Hail Mary . . .

7. When it says, "He ascended," what does it mean but that he had also descended into the lower parts of the earth? *(Ephesians 4:9)*

Hail Mary . . .

8. He who descended is the same one who ascended far above all the heavens, so that he might fill all things. *(Ephesians 4:10)*

Hail Mary . . .

9. He entered once for all into the Holy Place, not with the blood of goats and calves, but with his own blood, thus obtaining eternal redemption. *(Hebrews 9:12)*

Hail Mary . . .

10. Christ did not enter a sanctuary made by human hands, a mere copy of the true one, but he entered into heaven itself, now to appear in the presence of God on our behalf. *(Hebrews 9:24)*

Hail Mary . . .
Glory Be . . .

Pentecost

Our Father...

1. When the day of Pentecost had come, they were all together in one place. *(Acts 2:1)*

   Hail Mary...

2. Suddenly from heaven there came a sound like the rush of a violent wind, and it filled the entire house where they were sitting. *(Acts 2:2)*

   Hail Mary...

3. Divided tongues, as of fire, appeared among them, and a tongue rested on each of them. *(Acts 2:3)*

   Hail Mary...

4. All of them were filled with the Holy Spirit and began to speak in other languages, as the Spirit gave them ability. *(Acts 2:4)*

   Hail Mary...

5. Peter, standing with the eleven, raised his voice and addressed the crowd, saying, "Let this be known to you, and listen to what I say." *(Acts 2:14)*

   Hail Mary...

6. David spoke of the resurrection of the Messiah, saying, He was not abandoned to Hades, nor did his flesh experience corruption. *(Acts 2:31)*

Hail Mary . . .

7. "Let the entire house of Israel know with certainty that God has made him both Lord and Messiah, this Jesus whom you crucified." *(Acts 2:36)*

Hail Mary . . .

8. When the crowd heard this, they were cut to the heart and said to Peter and to the other apostles, "Brothers, what should we do?" *(Acts 2:37)*

Hail Mary . . .

9. Peter said to them, "Repent, and be baptized every one of you in the name of Jesus Christ so that your sins may be forgiven; and you will receive the gift of the Holy Spirit." *(Acts 2:38)*

Hail Mary . . .

10. Those who welcomed his message were baptized, and that day about three thousand persons were added. *(Acts 2:41)*

Hail Mary . . .
Glory Be . . .

The Assumption

Our Father . . .

1. Rise up, O Lord, and go to your resting place, you and the ark of your might. *(Psalm 132:8)*

> *Hail Mary . . .*

2. My beloved speaks and says to me: "Arise, my love, my fair one, and come away." *(Songs 2:10)*

> *Hail Mary . . .*

3. "And if I go and prepare a place for you, I will come again and will take you to myself, so that where I am, there you may be also." *(John 14:3)*

> *Hail Mary . . .*

4. The woman was given the two wings of the great eagle, so that she could fly from the serpent into the wilderness, to her place where she is nourished. *(Revelation 12:14)*

> *Hail Mary . . .*

5. For she is a reflection of eternal light, a spotless mirror of the working God, and an image of his goodness. *(Wisdom of Solomon 7:26)*

> *Hail Mary . . .*

6. "You are the exultation of Jerusalem, you are the great glory of Israel, you are the great pride of our nation! ... You have done great good to Israel, and God is well pleased with it. May the Almighty Lord bless you forever!" *(Judith 15:9–10)*

> *Hail Mary . . .*

7. Draw me after you, let us make haste. The king has brought me into his chambers. *(Songs 1:4)*

> *Hail Mary . . .*

8. "O daughter, you are blessed by the Most High God above all other women on earth." *(Judith 13:18)*

> *Hail Mary . . .*

9. "May God grant this to be a perpetual honor to you, and may he reward you with blessings." *(Judith 13:20)*

> *Hail Mary . . .*

10. Surely, from now on all generations will call Mary blessed. *(Luke 1:48)*

> *Hail Mary . . .*
> *Glory Be . . .*

The Crowning of Mary Queen of Heaven

Our Father . . .

1. When the chief shepherd appears, you will win the crown of glory that never fades away. *(1 Peter 5:4)*

   Hail Mary . . .

2. Be faithful until death, and I will give you the crown of life. *(Revelation 2:10)*

   Hail Mary . . .

3. To the one who conquers I will give a place with me on my throne, just as I myself conquered and sat down with my Father on his throne. *(Revelation 3:21)*

   Hail Mary . . .

4. The king rose to meet her, and bowed down to her; then he sat on his throne, and had a throne brought for the king's mother, and she sat on his right. *(1 Kings 2:19)*

   Hail Mary . . .

5. At your right hand stands the queen in gold. *(Psalm 45:9)*

   Hail Mary . . .

6. I dwelt in the highest heavens, and my throne was in a pillar of cloud. *(Sirach 24:4)*

Hail Mary . . .

7. My God has clothed me with the garments of salvation, he has covered me with the robe of righteousness. *(Isaiah 61:10)*

Hail Mary . . .

8. From now on there is reserved for me the crown of righteousness. *(2 Timothy 4:8)*

Hail Mary . . .

9. "Who is this that looks forth like the dawn, fair as the moon, bright as the sun, terrible as an army with banners?" *(Songs 6:10)*

Hail Mary . . .

10. A great portent appeared in heaven: a woman clothed with the sun, with the moon under her feet, and on her head a crown of twelve stars. *(Revelation 12:1)*

Hail Mary . . .
Glory Be . . .

PART
FOUR

Every Family Needs a Prayerful Giant

Over the years I have encountered many great families in my travels. A number of years ago, I started trying to work out what made these families so steadfast and full of life. Tolstoy begins the epic novel *Anna Karenina* with these lines: "Happy families are all alike; every unhappy family is unhappy in its own way." What I have discovered is that all the great families I have encountered have a prayerful giant, a person who covers his or her family with prayer, anchoring the family in God's grace. These prayerful giants pray constantly for their families, surrounding them with God's protection. Somewhere in each great family's not-too-distant past is a person who was a prayerful giant. Sometimes it is the grandmother or grandfather, the mother or father, an uncle or aunt, and from time to time you have to go back two or three generations, sometimes more. But you always find a prayerful giant in their family tree. Every family needs a cornerstone of prayer to pray for the family, now and in the future.

I suppose if a family gets far enough down the road from that prayerful giant without raising up another, its members begin to lose their way. Does it take a generation or two, or three or four? I don't know. I suppose it depends on many variables. But in each generation, each family needs at least one of these men and women of faithful prayer to guide and protect it.

It has always amazed me that when I am writing a book, a number of people and experiences cross my path to fill in the gaps. It is almost as if God were whispering in my ear. As I was working on a draft of this chapter, I had one of those moments. I was at dinner in Los Angeles, and I asked my hosts some questions about themselves and their lives. What I heard was the story of a prayerful giant.

My curiosity was piqued when I discovered that my hosts have six children and twenty-two grandchildren, and they are all practicing Catholics. Wherever I go, I encounter parents and grandparents who are heartbroken because their children or grandchildren have left the Church. So I wondered who were the prayerful giants in the past and the present of this family. My hosts were Kathleen and Allen Lund. This is Kathleen's father's story.

On the afternoon of January 24, 1945, American soldier Eddy Baranski was executed at the Nazi concentration camp in Mauthausen after being brutally tortured for days. He was a son, a husband, and a father. His father never spoke his son's name again for the rest of his life. His mother prayed for her boy every day for as long as she lived. His young wife, Madeline, had a vision of him smiling at her, at what she would later learn was the very moment of his death. And his daughter, Kathleen, who was just two years old when her daddy went off to fight Hitler, spent the next fifty years fatherless, unable to remember his voice, his touch, or his smell.

Fifty years later Kathleen's daughter participated in a study abroad program in Austria, and while visiting her Kathleen decided to go to Mauthausen. There she stood in the basement where her father had been tortured and shot in the head. She stood there as if waiting for something—some feeling, some message—but there was nothing.

Returning home, Kathleen began inquiring more about her father. She spoke with relatives, wrote to the National Archives, to museums in Europe, and to the United States Army, and slowly, the story of a father she had never known began to emerge.

In 1945 Werner Muller, a German citizen, dictated an extraordinary document to an Austrian lieutenant. The multilingual Werner had worked as an interpreter under Heinrich Himmler. In October 1944 Muller was ordered to Mauthausen, where his job was to translate the interrogations of Allied prisoners. He described the next three months as a living hell. Muller remembered one prisoner above all: Eddy Baranski.

He described Baranski praying as a group of Nazi officers tortured him. The commandant asked the interpreter what he was saying, and when Muller revealed that he was praying, the officers all burst into laughter. They then offered him a drink by placing water on a table, but the torture had left him incapable of raising his arms or hands, and they would not raise the water to his mouth. Muller described this as the most miserable afternoon of his life.

Little by little, the story of the father she had lost so early in life was coming together for Kathleen. A couple of years later, she visited Piest, Slovakia, where her father had been captured, and the house where he was living at the time of his arrest. There she met Maria Lakotova, who wept when she remembered Eddy Baranski, who used to sing lullabies to her at night when she was a young child in that house.

"Your father would hold me. I would sit on his knees and he would sing to me," Maria told Kathleen. "But I know he was not singing to me; he was singing to you, his little girl so far away."

Kathleen never knew it, but her father was singing to her—and praying for her. Eddy Baranski was a prayerful giant. Every family needs at least one. Today Allen and Kathleen are continuing the legacy by praying for their children and grandchildren each day.

Every family needs a prayerful giant, and parishes are like large families in many ways. Every parish needs some prayerful giants to surround the parish with prayer. Our world is racing more and more toward becoming an individualistic world, and the parish is one of the casualties of this rampant focus on self. Many people come to Mass on Sunday but never participate beyond that. They don't engage the community, and the community doesn't engage them. Furthermore, they can often come and go on a Sunday without speaking to anybody else except during the sign of peace. It is, for these people, a wholly personal experience devoid of communal meaning. To explore how far-reaching this attitude might be, ask yourself: What percentage of your parishioners have prayed for the parish outside of the Mass in the past thirty days? This is one of the highest indicators of engagement. We have not conducted research on this question yet, but you can be sure it is a very, very small percentage. Like families, parishes need giants of prayer to guide and protect them.

Have you ever known a really prayerful person? What did you notice about that person? Your family, your parish, the Church, and the world need you to become a prayerful giant.

Allow me to repeat something that I said earlier. I encourage you to begin (or renew) your commitment to a life of prayer today. Use the Rosary and The Prayer Process to guide you. If you do, I am confident that you will find they are faithful guides that will lead you deep into a lifelong friendship with God. What are you going to do in this life that is more fulfilling than developing a friendship with God? One of the great moments in the life of a Christian comes when we realize, once and for all, that a life of prayer is better than a life without it.

Your family needs a prayerful giant. Decide right now to accept God's invitation and challenge to become your family's prayerful giant. Start praying for everyone in your extended family. But don't stop there. Research your family tree, and start praying for generations past, as far back as you can trace. And start praying for future generations—pray for the next ten generations and beyond.

Most of us pray in a very limited way, confined to the here and now. As we grow spiritually, the Holy Spirit teaches us that the geography of our prayer should reach out to every corner of the earth and beyond, and that our prayer is not limited to this place and time; it can reach way back to past generations and well into the future to generations of people we will never meet or know in this life.

The spiritual life is an endless opportunity to love.

Beautifully Aware

Over the past few years, I have noticed that people in social settings—old friends and new—are more comfortable asking me questions about my writings. Sometimes the questions come from a place of skepticism; other times they come from a genuine desire to know. But whether the person asking the questions is aware of it or not, these questions always represent a hunger we all have. From the beginning, humanity has been trying to work out the best way to live. The great philosophers of every age have obsessed themselves with the question, and ordinary people like you and me grapple with it every single day of our lives in very practical ways.

"Why do you pray?" is a question I get often. In our increasingly secular culture, a growing number of people seem perplexed by anyone who is able to participate at a high level in business, academics, politics, or science and at the same time place enduring values supported by regular prayer at the center of their lives.

I love prayer. I don't know how people live without it. Still, I wish I had the time and the discipline to pray a lot more. Toward the end of each year, as I reflect on the year that has been and the year that is ahead, I almost always hope and resolve to pray more in the coming year.

Why do I pray? I pray because I cannot live without it. Not happily, anyway. I suppose what I am trying to say is that I can survive without prayer, but I cannot *thrive* without it.

Prayer is essential. It cuts through and clarifies. Prayer helps me to discover who I am, what I am here for, what matters most, and what matters least. By reminding me of what is really important, prayer teaches me to make great decisions. Just like love, prayer rearranges our priorities.

Prayer awakens me to what I really need in order to thrive. It points out that wants are good and wonderful and a gift from God, but our needs are more important. God loves order, and from that order flows peace, joy, and clarity. Prayer reminds me that needs are primary and wants are secondary, and that there is an order to everything. It cautions me to remember that getting what you want doesn't necessarily make you happy, because you simply never can get enough of what you don't really need.

Prayer is the great friend who introduces us to ourselves. It is the great mediator who introduces us to God. Prayer is the faithful friend who points out who we are and who we are capable of being, and encourages or challenges us to become a-better-version-of-ourselves.

Prayer reveals the deepest desires of our hearts and points out the path that was ordained for us from the beginning of time. It whispers those golden words, "That is your star; go now and follow it." The passion, purpose, and direction that we all yearn for are just some of the fruits of prayer.

Prayer is a journey and a destination. It is a chance to become intimately familiar with the better person we know we can be—and that self-knowledge is the beginning of wisdom.

Prayer is important. It helps. It works. It is needed. I need it. Prayer doesn't need me, and God doesn't need prayer. It doesn't help God; it helps us. It isn't something we must do. It is something we get to do, and until we see that, it is something we should do.

I pray because I cannot help it. I pray because in every moment the need to do so flows out of me. I pray because I am a better person when I do. I cannot imagine a life without prayer. I'd go crazy. That's not hyperbole or an attention-grabbing exaggeration. I think I would literally go crazy if I were prevented from praying.

Prayer makes me a better person. It makes me a better friend, a better father, a better husband, a better son and brother, a better employer and leader, a better citizen of this country, and a better member of the human family. Prayer makes me a-better-version-of-myself.

But let me caution you: Prayer is difficult. At first you may feel like you are floating on clouds, but over time, as you work to establish a consistent daily routine of prayer, you will be tempted at every turn to procrastinate and delay it, or neglect it altogether. The person who prays every day is a force to be reckoned with. The man or woman who prays every day will change every person and place his or her path crosses. So, let me say this just once. I rarely speak of such things, because it is a topic that most concerns the spiritually mature. Any evil thing or person and whatever evil spirits are at work in this world will do everything within their considerable power to ensure you don't establish a deep and consistent daily habit of prayer.

Prayer is difficult. One of the greatest difficulties is that any form of spiritual exercise brings us face-to-face with who we are: strengths and weaknesses, faults, failings, flaws, defects, hopes and dreams, and the lies. What lies? The lies we tell ourselves about ourselves. Prayer strips all this away, and that can be quite scary. Don't let these truths discourage you. I just want you to be able to recognize what is happening when these things rear their ugly heads along your journey.

Beyond the question of why I pray, people also especially ask why I pray the Rosary. As I have already articulated briefly, one of the main reasons I pray the Rosary is because it works. It just works, and I love that. Perhaps I'm not smart enough to think about it in ways that are theological and philosophical, but even if I were, I believe I would still value the practicality of this powerful spiritual exercise beyond the theology of it.

So, I just keep coming back to that. It works. But I really hope you won't take my word for it. I want you to try it for yourself. It just works, and it will change your life in unimaginable ways.

I could try to explain it, and I suppose in many ways this book has been making a case for the Rosary, but at the end of the day, it impacts people's lives in different ways, and it impacts the same person's life in different ways at different stages. So I am mindful and hesitant to describe what I know it has done for other people because this might create expectations in you, while God may be planning to use the Rosary in a completely different way in your life.

But let me share some of the general ways it has impacted my life and the lives of many people I know. When I make the effort to create a place and a space to pray the Rosary, it fills me with an incredible peace. Now, there are some days when I am too distracted to accept this peace. But when I am in the right state of mind, the Rosary unfailingly delivers a peace that nothing in this world seems to give me.

The Rosary teaches me to let go and surrender, calms me down when I am all worked up about something, and teaches me to slow down and put things in perspective. The Rosary is an antidote. It is all the things busy modern people need.

STEP BACK AND GET A LITTLE PERSPECTIVE

From time to time we all need to step back from who we are, where we are, and what we're doing, and reassess who we are and what on earth we are doing. It's important because we won't be here long. If we don't make an effort to step back regularly, the momentum of life can carry us away, and before long we don't even recognize ourselves. Then we run the risk of waking up one morning with the feeling that we are living someone else's life.

You could go on retreat for a couple of days once a year, and that would be powerful. You could make a pilgrimage to one of the epic holy places of our faith. I've seen this change so many people's lives—and my own too. But time passes between these experiences, and we can easily lose God's perspective. The Rosary is a mini-retreat. The Rosary is a pilgrimage in your pocket.

Do you ever feel like stepping back from the world? Do you ever feel like taking a nice, long, extended break from the daily commitments and responsibilities of life? I sure do. Airports and hotels; crowds of people; project deadlines; getting pulled in so many different directions; the unexpected stuff that just happens, which you cannot plan for or schedule. I get this feeling every couple of years. I push myself too hard, commit to too many things, get overwhelmed and a little bit burned out . . . and then I just want to run away and take a break. If you ever feel like running away from the world and just leaving everything behind, going somewhere quiet and simple, the Rosary is a great way to do that.

I yearn for peace. We all do, I think. It is good to get away from time to time and go off on a retreat or pilgrimage. But we also need to find ways to connect with that feeling of stepping back from it all each day. It doesn't come naturally for me. I have to work at it. By nature or nurture—I don't know which—I am restless. I like to be on the move, doing things, making things happen, and I have a hard time just sitting down and relaxing. So, I have to continue to work at being still and quiet, and it is not a lesson once learned. It is a lesson I have to learn over and over again.

I have learned to find peace by taking long walks in quiet places. That peace is there for a fleeting moment when my children hug me, and I find myself hoping they will hold on just that little bit longer. When one of my children falls asleep in my arms, that is something amazing—my heart fills with a deep peace and contentment, and I cannot help but turn to God with a grateful heart and then ask him to watch over my children. I find these same experiences of peace when I pray the Rosary.

Praying the Rosary is like stepping back from the crazy, noisy, busy world and into a calm, quiet, peaceful haven.

ONE COLOSSAL BENEFIT OF THE ROSARY

My father was an entrepreneur and a salesman. "How do you sell stuff to people, Dad?" I'd ask. "Well, the best thing to do is to have a good product, then you find someone who needs that product. Then explain the benefits of your product and how it will make their business and life better." My dad liked to say, "A sale is just a logical conclusion to a rational conversation."

We have spoken about a variety of benefits that flow from praying the Rosary regularly. But as we come toward the end of our time together, let's discuss just one astounding benefit and gift that comes from praying the Rosary. It is a benefit that is almost never mentioned, but it is a giant one, and it is central to a rich and vibrant spiritual life.

This giant benefit of the Rosary is awareness. Being aware of what is happening inside, around, and to us is one of the most incredible gifts God can give us.

Think about something as simple as scheduling. Do you ever put things on your schedule and then later wonder why you did it? It's as if you weren't even aware of what you were doing at the time. The Rosary fills you with an awareness that poses questions while things are actually happening. How do you feel about putting that event on your schedule? God is saying something to you through that feeling. But are you aware? The feeling could be excitement and anticipation, or it could be dread. Either way, God is speaking to you, guiding you, and trying to counsel you about the best way to proceed. The super-aware Christian takes a moment to think about this before committing to anything.

We all get put on the spot to agree to do something or attend some event. How often do you say yes to something under pressure and then regret it later? The aware person doesn't let that happen. The aware person is ready for that situation and has prepared an answer for situations just like it.

"Jim, I'm not sure if I can, but shoot me an email and I will check my schedule and get back to you quickly." Now, occasionally you will come up against someone who is particularly pushy. He is probably a great salesman. The super-aware person has an answer prepared: "Jim, if you have to have an answer right now, the answer has to be no. I'm sorry."

One of the rarest gifts that awareness freely gives us is the ability to see things as they really are. How many people do you know who see things as they really are? So many people are over-opinionated. People have opinions about stuff they know nothing about. As soon as they start speaking, it is clear they have no idea what they are talking about.

In order to see things as they really are, we need to grapple with four of life's perennial questions: Who am I? What am I here for? What matters most? What matters least?

Wrestling with these questions throughout our lives helps us to develop astounding personal clarity. This clarity helps us to see every invitation and opportunity as it really is. This extraordinary clarity is a finely tuned form of awareness and tends to make those who possess it very good decision makers. They are typically very decisive; they don't waver; they act from clarity and don't look back.

We develop this awareness by looking deeper into the details of the mysteries. Look at Jesus' sandals as he stands speaking to a crowd, notice the dust on them, and you are already on a completely different plane of awareness. And that is a plane that most people never stumble upon, one that most have never been taught about.

All the many ways we pray and reflect upon the Rosary help us grow in awareness.

Praying the Rosary regularly also encourages us to slow down, which in turn should encourage us to live life at a different pace than the rest of the world. This slower pace allows us to be present.

If you meet any deeply spiritual person, a holy person, one thing you will discover is that she is present to you. For the few seconds or minutes that you are with her, she gives you her full attention. It is as if nothing else exists but the two of you. At the same time, be aware enough to know that even people living heroically holy lives have bad days. So if someone you consider holy seems distracted, give him the benefit of the doubt. Like us all, he might just be having a bad day.

How present are you? When your spouse is speaking to you, are you present? Are you 100 percent present to your children when you are with them? When you take a day off or go on vacation, do you turn your phone off and leave your work at home? When the answer to these questions is no—when you're thinking about something else or are enslaved to the device, for example— you divide yourself. A divided self is a recipe for dissatisfaction and misery. Nothing good can come from a divided self. And a divided self is never truly present to anything or anyone.

Young employees at Dynamic Catholic, or at the other businesses I am involved in, often come to me and ask: How do I get ahead here? I always tell them the same thing: Be present to whatever your leader is asking you to do right now. Crush what you are doing right now. That's the best way to rise in the organization. Look around at the leadership team—that's how they got there. They crushed the first thing we put in front of them, then we gave them something bigger or more important, and they crushed that. They were 100 percent present to their current assignment.

Learn to be 100 percent present to whomever and whatever is in front of you right now. The Rosary will teach you if you don't rush it too much.

Once Jesus and Mary teach us to see things as they really are, they move us to a doctorate-level awareness: experiencing things as they really are. God wants you to taste every mouthful of food and soak in every awe-inspiring scene in nature.

He wants you to wake up, so you can experience life in every breath. This heightened awareness makes food taste different. With this awareness, just washing your hands in clean, fresh water can be a powerful moment.

Most people have very, very little awareness. Most people are sleepwalking through life. It is one of the great tragedies of our age. God wants to teach us to see, hear, touch, and taste differently. He wants us to see not just with the eyes in our head but also with the eyes of our soul. When we do, what we see is vastly different. William Blake wrote: "To see a World in a Grain of Sand / And a Heaven in a Wild Flower / Hold Infinity in the palm of your hand / And Eternity in an hour."

When your five-year-old daughter or granddaughter comes running up to you filled with pure delight and gives you the hugest hug her little self is capable of, God wants you fully present. He wants you to experience that for the miracle it is. He wants you to lose yourself in that hug. The temptation is to try to hold on to it, but that takes you out of the moment. God wants you to be radically present.

Next Sunday when you walk down the aisle to receive Jesus in the Eucharist, God wants your heart, mind, body, and soul to be fully present. He wants you to conjure up the story of the woman who was dying until she touched the Master's cloak. She had a terminal disease and was healed just by touching his cloak. You are about to receive the real Jesus—body, blood, soul, and divinity. You are going to consume him. With an open heart, the impact of receiving Jesus in the Eucharist just once is incalculable. But we are asleep. If you watch people standing in line to receive Communion, they are in a trancelike state. That's not a spiritual thing; it's a worldly trance. They are asleep. They are sleepwalking through life.

If you want to chase something, chase down spiritual and emotional awareness. If you want to ask God for something, ask for awareness. If you want to obsess about something, get obsessed with awareness. How? Awareness is the fruit of prayer.

All forms of prayer change the way we see things. Prayer changes the ways we see ourselves, God, the world, our family, the past and present events of our lives, and so much more. But the Rosary is especially effective and powerful at awakening this astounding awareness in people.

THE MOMENT AND THIS MOMENT

What are some of the most important moments in history? Ask any group of people this question and you are sure to have an interesting discussion. First, you will notice that most people pick a moment that relates to themselves in some way, even if that simply means a sporting event in which their team won. Most people's selections will say more about them than about the question itself. Unless we have the awareness not to, we see everything and everyone, including history, through the lens of self.

There is one moment that most likely will not be mentioned. It doesn't matter if you are among the well educated or those with very little education; they miss it almost all the time. It is one of the epic moments in history. It's a moment I spend a lot of time thinking about: Mary's moment, the Annunciation. She was a teenager, just a child. She was alone. And what the angel was saying made no worldly sense. It was a quiet moment. There was no cheering, no banners, and no media. The angel made her feel very peaceful, but I am sure that dissipated after he left and Mary started thinking about how she was going to tell people. Who would ever believe her? Would Joachim and Anne believe her? Would her fiancé, Joseph, believe her? What would people in the village think and say? Was her life in danger? Would they try to stone her?

This is the most astounding pregnancy ever. Imagine if Joseph had said, "No, I just can't do this." Nobody could have blamed him. And again there is that thing we call free will. Mary could've been a single mother.

Imagine the monumental courage that would have been required. Again, she was little more than a child, yet she had a very well-developed sense of self, a rare intimacy with God, and more awareness and wisdom than anyone before her. All these helped her to recognize the import of the moment.

But think about it. Everything hung in the balance. And don't forget free will, a necessary ingredient for all true love—and what Mary was agreeing to was true love. Imagine the anticipation in heaven. Every angel on the edge of their seats. Waiting. Waiting. Hurry up. Gabriel, get to the point! All the angels and all of history were waiting. Gabriel got to the point, but then Mary wanted to ask questions. The waiting must have seemed eternal. Everything hung in the balance.

What would have happened if Mary had said no? We will never know. Just as we will never know what might have happened if we had said yes to God that time we said no.

She said yes. One epic yes. One word. Well, I suppose she used seventeen words. But it was a wholehearted yes for God. Heaven must have exploded with praise and rejoicing. All because of the faith of a little girl named Miriam. It was an epic moment in history. And it is a moment that echoes throughout every age.

Growing up in Australia, I attended an all-boys' Catholic high school. Every day at noon, the whole campus came to a standstill. If you were moving from one building to another, you were expected to stop exactly where you were at that moment. Failure to do so meant certain detention. The principal then led the whole school, more than twelve hundred boys, in praying the Angelus. It seems extraordinary to me looking back twenty-five years. Some days we would pay more attention than on other days. And there were days we no doubt saw it as an inconvenience, an obstacle to whatever was next in our very important, very busy lives. There was very little awareness going around at that time among my peers and me, but the experience taught us all something—many things, I suspect. For the rest of my life, that is the only thing I will ever think about at noon.

The intercom blasted into each classroom and every outdoor space on campus. If you were on the football or cricket field, you knew and could hear clearly. Then we prayed, recalling this epic moment in history. No doubt our teachers were praying and hoping that we would say yes to God in our own way as we got older.

Our teachers made clear that this was a sacred moment, and the principal would begin:

The Angel of the Lord declared to Mary:
R. And she conceived of the Holy Spirit.

Hail Mary . . .

Behold the handmaid of the Lord:
R. Be it done unto me according to your word.

Hail Mary . . .

And the Word became Flesh:
R. And dwelt among us.

Hail Mary . . .

Pray for us, O Holy Mother of God,
R. That we may be made worthy of the promises of Christ.

Let Us Pray:
Pour forth, we beseech you, O Lord, your grace into our hearts; that we, to whom the incarnation of Jesus, your Son, was made known by the message of an angel, may by His Passion and Cross be brought to the glory of His Resurrection, through the same Christ Our Lord. *Amen.*

It was over in a couple of minutes; the prayer is beautiful in its simplicity. But it was powerful, as demonstrated by how impactful the memory of that experience is twenty-five years later.

Ritual, routine, regular habits, and sacred moments are so important. Without them we can survive—miserably—but we cannot thrive without them.

WHY NOW?

As I mentioned earlier, my first book was about the Rosary. I wrote it when I was eighteen, and it was published a year or so later. When Pope John Paul II added the Luminous Mysteries in 2002, I decided to add reflections on those mysteries, but as I started to work on it I realized there was so much to the book that I wanted to change. So I set the project aside, many times trying to come back to it, but putting it off for other projects—until now.

Why now? I really don't know. I like to say that books have a life of their own and you cannot force it. This is a better, richer book for my having waited to work on it; I know that for sure.

This year, 2017, is the one hundredth anniversary of the first apparition in Fatima, so perhaps that has something to do with it. I have always been drawn to Fatima, and drawn to Our Lady of Fatima. Her message was so simple and so practical: Pray and fast, for yourself, for others, and for the world. In all my travels, I have never visited the other major Marian sites around the world, but I have been to Fatima more than twenty times. Most of these trips were made with about a hundred pilgrims, and it was a real privilege to see their lives change through the encounter.

Why now? One hundred years ago the world was in bad shape in a lot of ways. Little did they know that the world was embarking on a century of war. These wars killed tens of millions, but even those who did come home would never be the same. War changes people, and it changed their marriages, families, neighborhoods, and society.

The world is certainly in a very fragile place again, one hundred years later. I know I could use a lot more prayer and fasting, and I don't need to be a prophet to realize that our current culture is running up spiritual debt even faster than it is increasing its financial debt—and that is saying something. The whole world and everyone in it needs prayer and fasting.

Why now? Probably for some reason I am not aware of, and I am OK with that. I have enjoyed writing this book. It has renewed my love of this powerful ancient prayer.

But it is getting late, and I sense that this book is now finished, so I must let go. It's a difficult thing to do, surrendering a book.

In my 1993 volume of reflections about the mysteries of the Rosary I opened the book with the following words. They now seem more appropriate at the end of this book.

> The days and weeks go by and life takes shape in a different way for each and every single one of us. But we all share the struggle to achieve as much good as we can in our one short lifetime, in this beautiful world that God in His goodness and generosity has entrusted to us. So when I lay my head on the pillow at night, it's important to be able to feel that something worthwhile has been achieved today.
>
> Our lives are a collection of days, a collection of moments. Each day and in each moment, we are called to say "yes" to God. In the First Mystery of the Rosary Mary teaches us how to respond humbly to the will of God, it's a lesson that I must ponder one more time before I add tomorrow's moments to my life.
>
> *Matthew Kelly*
> Written in Sydney, Australia,
> on July 29, the Feast of Saint Martha,
> in the year 1993.

I will fall asleep with my rosary beads tonight—one more reason I love my simple wooden rosary. It occurs to me that the reason this wooden rosary is my favorite is probably because it is very practical. It doesn't break, it doesn't get all tangled up, and it doesn't scratch or cut me in the night if I fall asleep with it. It is my favorite because I am a practical man: I love things that work.

The Rosary works. I don't know if you read this book to rediscover the Rosary and rekindle the practice in your life. I don't know if you read it to discover the Rosary because for whatever reason it has never been part of your prayer life. And maybe you are somewhere in between. Regardless, I hope you have found in these pages a little more inspiration than you expected, and plenty of practical ways to enrich your experience of the ancient and epic prayer we call the Rosary.

So grab your favorite rosary and get busy. Your family needs a prayerful giant, and the world needs men and women of deep prayer.

ONE LAST QUESTION

For almost a decade when I first started speaking and writing, I had a fabulous spiritual director. He was a happy man. He was a holy man—and I do not say that lightly. He had an amazing smile. He would tell me something that was tough love and something I really needed to hear, and then he would just smile at me with all the love in the world.

He was an incredible spiritual director because he had no agenda. He didn't want anything from me. His only goal was to help me grow spiritually, so I could discover and do God's will. Everything else was secondary.

Every week when I met with him, he started with exactly the same question: How's your prayer life? Today, I ask you the same question. Give yourself a score between 1 and 10. How is your prayer life? What are you going to do today to move the needle?

Pray the Rosary. Brother, sister, pray the Rosary—and remember me in your prayers when you do.

I hope you have enjoyed

Rediscover the Rosary

It has been a great privilege to write for you.
May God bless you with a prayerful spirit
and a peaceful heart.

MATTHEW KELLY

APPENDICES

The Basics: How to Pray the Rosary

I have placed these simple directions about how to pray the Rosary at the back of this volume because I suspect the majority of people who would pick up a book like this already know how to pray the Rosary. At the same time there is an increasing number of people of all ages who have never been taught to pray it, and if you are one of them, I hope this simple guide serves you in a very practical way.

With the Rosary losing popularity in recent decades, there are many more people who simply don't know how to pray it. During this period we have also seen an increase in the number of converts to Catholicism from other Christian churches, and these converts in many cases also have never been taught to pray the Rosary.

This section is included for those people, but also as a step-by-step guide for parents and grandparents who wish to teach their children and grandchildren how to pray the Rosary.

THE FOUR THINGS YOU NEED TO KNOW TO PRAY THE ROSARY

1. The prayers
2. The mysteries
3. The rosary beads
4. How the beads are used

THE PRAYERS OF THE ROSARY

The Sign of the Cross
In the name of the Father, and of the Son, and of the Holy Spirit. *Amen.*

The Apostles' Creed
I believe in God, the Father almighty, Creator of heaven and earth, and in Jesus Christ, his only Son, our Lord, who was conceived by the Holy Spirit, born of the Virgin Mary, suffered under Pontius Pilate, was crucified, died, and was buried; he descended into hell; on the third day he rose again from the dead; he ascended into heaven, and is seated at the right hand of God the Father almighty; from there he will come to judge the living and the dead. I believe in the Holy Spirit, the holy catholic Church, the communion of saints, the forgiveness of sins, the resurrection of the body, and life everlasting. *Amen.*

Our Father
Our Father, who art in heaven, hallowed be thy name. Thy kingdom come, thy will be done on earth as it is in heaven. Give us this day our daily bread, and forgive us our trespasses, as

we forgive those who trespass against us. And lead us not into temptation, but deliver us from evil. *Amen.*

Hail Mary

Hail Mary, full of grace, the Lord is with thee. Blessed art thou among women, and blessed is the fruit of thy womb, Jesus. Holy Mary, mother of God, pray for us sinners, now and at the hour of our death. *Amen.*

Glory Be

Glory be to the Father, and to the Son, and to the Holy Spirit, as it was in the beginning, is now and ever shall be, world without end. *Amen.*

The Fatima Prayer

O my Jesus, forgive us our sins, save us from the fires of hell. Lead all souls to heaven, especially those in most need of thy mercy.

*This is the prayer that was added in the early twentieth century in response to the vision of Fatima; it is an optional addition to the Rosary.

Hail Holy Queen

Hail Holy Queen, Mother of mercy, our life, our sweetness, and our hope. To thee do we cry, poor banished children of Eve. To thee do we send up our sighs, mourning and weeping in this valley of tears. Turn then, most gracious Advocate, thine eyes of mercy toward us. And, after this our exile, show unto us the blessed fruit of thy womb, Jesus. O clement, O loving, O sweet virgin Mary.

Pray for us, O holy mother of God
R. that we may be made worthy of the promises of Christ.

The Rosary Prayer

Let us pray.
R. O God, whose only-begotten Son by his life, death and resurrection, has purchased for us the rewards of eternal life; grant,
we beseech thee, that by meditating upon these mysteries of
the most holy Rosary of the Blessed Virgin Mary, we may imi-
tate what they contain and obtain what they promise, through
the same Christ our Lord. *Amen.*

*Note: People will sometimes add other prayers as well, but these
are the basic ones.*

THE MYSTERIES OF THE ROSARY

The Five Joyful Mysteries

The Annunciation
The Visitation
The Birth of Jesus
The Presentation
Finding the Child Jesus in the Temple

The Five Luminous Mysteries

The Baptism of Jesus in the River Jordan
The Wedding Feast at Cana
The Proclamation of the Kingdom of God
The Transfiguration of Jesus
The Institution of the Eucharist

The Five Sorrowful Mysteries

The Agony in the Garden
The Scourging at the Pillar
The Crowning with Thorns
The Carrying of the Cross
The Crucifixion of Jesus

The Five Glorious Mysteries

The Resurrection
The Ascension
Pentecost
The Assumption
The Crowning of Mary Queen of Heaven

The Joyful Mysteries are typically prayed on Monday and Saturday; the Luminous Mysteries on Thursday; the Sorrowful Mysteries on Tuesday and Friday; and the Glorious Mysteries on Wednesday and Sunday.

YOUR ROSARY BEADS

In my life, I have probably been gifted about a thousand rosaries. Most of them I have passed along to other people as gifts. There are all types of rosaries, from the simplest to the fanciest. I was once given a rosary made of solid gold as a thank-you gift for visiting the Cayman Islands. For about ten years I held on to it, until a bishop from a very poor diocese in Africa came to visit. Giving it to him, I explained what it was and said, "Keep it to pray with and to let your people pray with as a diocesan rosary, or sell it to pay for a priority need in your diocese. Either way I will know it has served your people, God's people, well."

There are, however, some rosaries that I have held on to, even though I never pray with them. First, there is the rosary that Mrs. Rutter gave me in fourth grade. It is a dark green knotted cord. In place of each bead is a knot, and it has a white plastic crucifix. It was made by an order of nuns in Papua New Guinea, a country in the South Pacific islands, just 125 miles off the northern tip of Australia. Then there are the rosaries given to me by Pope John Paul II and Pope Francis. But as I've said, the one I prefer to pray with is a simple wooden rosary. I have a lot of them: one in my bedside table, another in my car, one in my briefcase, one in my desk at the office, and another in my desk at home.

The beads make the Rosary a physical prayer as well as a spiritual prayer. The simple motion of moving your fingers from one bead to another creates a powerful rhythm. This physical motion and the rhythm it creates add to the soothing of your heart, mind, and soul that praying the Rosary produces.

Great music is not just about the notes; just as important are the spaces between the notes. The beads are important because they represent the prayers, but the spaces between the beads are important too. Breathe during those spaces and allow the powerful rhythm to build. Otherwise there can be a tendency to rush. Once we start racing through the prayers, something is lost.

How to Use the Beads

A rosary has fifty-nine beads. Each bead corresponds with a prayer; some beads correspond with more than one prayer. The Rosary is made up of five decades. Each decade consists of one Our Father, ten Hail Marys, and one Glory Be. These account for fifty-five beads. There are also four introductory beads and a crucifix.

Following is a step-by-step explanation of what prayer (or prayers) to pray as you hold each bead. I have also included a diagram to provide further clarity.

This prayer has changed millions of lives. It has been a staple prayer for countless saints. May it change your life, help you to become the-very-best-version-of-yourself, and lead you to grow in virtue and live a holy life.

BEAD BY BEAD

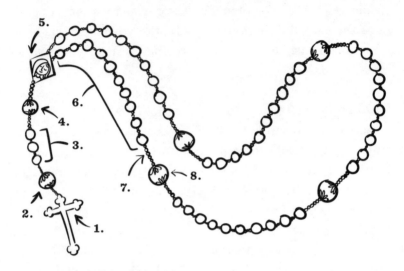

Introductory Prayers

1. Crucifix. Make the Sign of the Cross and pray the Apostles' Creed.
2. Pray the Our Father; traditionally this is prayed for the intentions of the pope and the needs of the Church.
3. Pray the Hail Mary on each bead; traditionally these have been prayed for an increase in the three theological virtues: faith, hope, and charity.
4. Pray the Glory Be.

The Five Decades/Mysteries

5. Pray the Our Father on the medal. (For the remaining four decades, pray the Our Father on the bead between the decades.)
6. Pray the Hail Mary on each bead.
7. Pray the Glory Be on the space after the tenth bead.

8. Pray the Fatima Prayer (optional).

9. Repeat steps 5 through 8 for each of the four remaining decades/mysteries.

Closing Prayers

10. Pray the Hail Holy Queen.

11. Pray the Rosary Prayer.

12. Make the Sign of the Cross.

Note: Visit DynamicCatholic.com/Joyful for a free audio version of the Joyful Mysteries. Praying with this recording will help you quickly pick up the practice and rhythm of the Rosary.

Quotes, Prayers, and Hymns About Mary and the Rosary

QUOTES ABOUT MARY AND THE ROSARY

"Pray, then let it go. Don't try and manipulate or force the outcome. Just trust God to open the right doors at the right time."
—Anonymous

"In times of darkness, holding the rosary beads is like holding Mary's hand." —Anonymous

"Nothing is so strong as gentleness. Nothing so gentle as real strength." —St. Francis de Sales

"The Rosary is the best therapy for these distraught, unhappy, fearful, and frustrated souls precisely because it involves the simultaneous use of three powers: the physical, the vocal, and the spiritual." —Venerable Fulton Sheen

"The Rosary was said every evening. I always liked that sentence about the medieval Churches, that they were the Bibles of the poor. The Church was my first book and I would think it is still my most important book." —John McGahern

"Never tire of praying ... it is what is essential." —St. Padre Pio

"When we have spiritual reading at meals, when we have study groups, forums, when we go out to distribute literature at meetings, or sell it on the street corners, Christ is there with us." —Dorothy Day

"Life is just better when you pray the Rosary." —Anonymous

"I thought that I had no time for faith, nor time to pray, then I saw an armless man saying his Rosary with his feet." —John Locke

"Every day I'm trying to be more humble and how do you do that? Every day, I pray the Rosary. That's what I do." —Jim Caviezel

"A world at prayer is a world at peace." —Father Patrick Peyton

"Abandon yourself into the arms of Mary. She will take care of you." —St. Padre Pio

"Amazing grace, how sweet thou art." —John Newton

"Let nothing trouble you.
Let nothing frighten you.
Everything passes.
God never changes.
Patience obtains all.

Whoever has God wants for nothing.
God alone is enough." —St. Teresa of Ávila

"I am a practical man. One of the reasons I love the Rosary is because it works. I love things that work. Pray the Rosary slowly, reflectively, and it will fill you with an incredible peace. But don't take my word for it. Try it for yourself." —Matthew Kelly

"No one can live continually in sin and continue to say the Rosary: either they will give up sin or they will give up the Rosary." —Bishop Hugh Boyle

"When God gives you a no, give him a thank-you. He was protecting you from less than his best." —Anonymous

"It is impossible to pray the Rosary regularly and not become a-better-version-of-yourself." —Matthew Kelly

"If you desire peace in your hearts, in your homes, and in your country, gather each evening to pray the Rosary. Let not even one day pass without saying it, no matter how burdened you may be with many cares of the world." —Pope Pius XI

"Where the Rosary is recited there will be days of peace and tranquility." —St. John Bosco

"There is evil in this world. I have seen it, been face-to-face with it, and experienced it. When you encounter raw evil, pray the Rosary." —Matthew Kelly

"Keep calm and pray the Rosary." —Anonymous

"When you realize how much God loves you, then you can only live your life radiating that love." —St. Teresa of Calcutta

"Every day I meet with Mary in the Rosary. I never neglect it, and she never neglects me." —St. John Paul II

"Mary's greatness consists in the fact that she wants to magnify God, not herself." —Pope Benedict XVI

"Anytime you feel yourself become discouraged, run to Mary, and she will fill you with hope again." —Matthew Kelly

"Mary pondered all these things in her heart." —Luke 2:19

"There is something immensely powerful about one person doing the right thing, at the right time, for the right reason. This is what Mary did, and it changed the world."
—Matthew Kelly

"Never be afraid of loving Mary too much. You can never love her more than Jesus did." —St. Maximilian Kolbe

"Let us live as Mary lived . . . loving God above all else, desiring God above all else, trying to please God above all else."
—St. John Vianney

"One thing that makes me strong every day is praying the Rosary." —Pope Francis

"Mary has produced, together with the Holy Spirit, the greatest thing which has been or ever will be—a God-Man; and she will consequently produce the greatest saints the world has ever seen." —St. Louis-Marie de Montfort

"The mysteries of the Rosary should be reproduced in our lives. Each mystery is a lesson in some virtue—particularly in the virtues of humility, trust, patience, and love."
—Father Reginald Garrigou-Lagrange, OP

"If priests and religious have an obligation to meditate on the great truths of our faith in order to live out their vocation worthily, then the same obligation is just as much incumbent upon the laity—because of the fact that every day they meet with spiritual dangers. Therefore they should meditate frequently on the life, virtues, and sufferings of Jesus—which are so beautifully contained in the mysteries of the Holy Rosary."
—St. Louis-Marie de Montfort

PRAYERS ABOUT MARY AND THE ROSARY

Hail Mary
Hail Mary, full of grace, the Lord is with thee.
Blessed art thou among women,
and blessed is the fruit of they womb, Jesus.
Holy Mary, mother of God, pray for us sinners,
now and at the hour of our death. *Amen.*

Hail Holy Queen
Hail holy queen, mother of mercy,
our life, our sweetness, and our hope.
To thee do we cry, poor banished children of Eve.
To thee do we send up our sighs,
mourning and weeping in this valley of tears.
Turn then, most gracious advocate,
thine eyes of mercy toward us.
And, after this our exile,
show unto us the blessed fruit of they womb, Jesus.
O clement, O loving, O sweet virgin Mary.

Magnificat
My soul proclaims the greatness of the Lord,
my spirit rejoices in God my Savior
for he has looked with favor on his lowly servant.
From this day all generations will call me blessed:
the Almighty has done great things for me,
and holy is his Name.

He has mercy on those who fear him
in every generation.

He has shown the strength of his arm,
he has scattered the proud in their conceit.

He has cast down the mighty from their thrones,
and has lifted up the lowly.
He has filled the hungry with good things,
and the rich he has sent away empty.
He has come to the help of his servant Israel
for he remembered his promise of mercy,
the promise he made to our fathers,
to Abraham and his children forever.

Memorare

Remember, O most gracious Virgin Mary, that never was it known that anyone who fled to thy protection, implored thy help, or sought thine intercession was left unaided. Inspired by this confidence, I fly unto thee, O Virgin of virgins, my mother; to thee do I come, before thee I stand, sinful and sorrowful. O Mother of the Word Incarnate, despise not my petitions, but in thy mercy hear and answer me. *Amen.*

Angelus

The Angel of the Lord declared to Mary:
R. And she conceived of the Holy Spirit.
Hail Mary, full of grace, the Lord is with thee; blessed art thou among women and blessed is the fruit of thy womb, Jesus. Holy Mary, Mother of God, pray for us sinners, now and at the hour of our death. *Amen.*

Behold the handmaid of the Lord:
R. Be it done unto me according to Thy word.

Hail Mary . . .

And the Word was made Flesh:
R. And dwelt among us.

Hail Mary . . .

Pray for us, O Holy Mother of God,
R. that we may be made worthy of the promises of Christ.

Let us pray:
Pour forth, we beseech Thee, O Lord, Thy grace into our hearts; that we, to whom the incarnation of Christ, Thy Son, was made known by the message of an angel, may by His Passion and Cross be brought to the glory of His Resurrection, through the same Christ Our Lord. *Amen.*

Miraculous Medal Prayer
O Mary, conceived without sin, pray for us who have recourse to thee, and for those who do not have recourse to thee, especially the enemies of the Church and those recommended to thee. *Amen.*

Litany of the Blessed Virgin Mary
Lord, have mercy on us.
Christ have mercy on us.
Lord, have mercy on us.
Christ, hear us.
Christ graciously hear us.
God the Father of Heaven,   have mercy on us.

God the Son, Redeemer of the world,	have mercy on us.
God the Holy Spirit,	have mercy on us.
Holy Trinity, One God,	have mercy on us.
Holy Mary,	pray for us.
Holy Mother of God,	pray for us.
Holy Virgin of virgins,	pray for us.
Mother of Christ,	pray for us.
Mother of divine grace,	pray for us.
Mother most pure,	pray for us.
Mother most chaste,	pray for us.
Mother inviolate,	pray for us.
Mother undefiled,	pray for us.
Mother most amiable,	pray for us.
Mother most admirable,	pray for us.
Mother of good counsel,	pray for us.
Mother of our Creator,	pray for us.
Mother of our Savior,	pray for us.
Mother of the Church,	pray for us.
Virgin most prudent,	pray for us.
Virgin most venerable,	pray for us.
Virgin most renowned,	pray for us.
Virgin most powerful,	pray for us.
Virgin most merciful,	pray for us.
Virgin most faithful,	pray for us.
Mirror of justice,	pray for us.
Seat of wisdom,	pray for us.
Cause of our joy,	pray for us.
Spiritual vessel,	pray for us.
Vessel of honor,	pray for us.
Singular vessel of devotion,	pray for us.

Mystical rose,	pray for us.
Tower of David,	pray for us.
Tower of ivory,	pray for us.
House of gold,	pray for us.
Ark of the covenant,	pray for us.
Gate of Heaven,	pray for us.
Morning star,	pray for us.
Health of the sick,	pray for us.
Refuge of sinners,	pray for us.
Comforter of the afflicted,	pray for us.
Help of Christians,	pray for us.
Queen of angels,	pray for us.
Queen of patriarchs,	pray for us.
Queen of prophets,	pray for us.
Queen of apostles,	pray for us.
Queen of martyrs,	pray for us.
Queen of confessors,	pray for us.
Queen of virgins,	pray for us.
Queen of all saints,	pray for us.
Queen conceived without Original Sin,	pray for us.
Queen assumed into Heaven,	pray for us.
Queen of the holy Rosary,	pray for us.
Queen of families,	pray for us.
Queen of peace,	pray for us.

Lamb of God, Who takes away the sins of the world
R. Spare us, O Lord.

Lamb of God, Who takes away the sins of the world,
R. Graciously spare us, O Lord.
Lamb of God, Who takes away the sins of the world,

R. Have mercy on us.

Pray for us, O Holy Mother of God,
R. That we may be worthy of the promises of Christ.

Let us pray:
Grant, we beseech Thee, O Lord God, that we Thy servants may enjoy perpetual health of mind and body, and by the glorious intercession of the Blessed Mary, ever Virgin, be delivered from present sorrow and enjoy everlasting happiness. Through Christ Our Lord. *Amen.*

HYMNS ABOUT MARY AND THE ROSARY

Hail Mary: Gentle Woman
by Carey Landry

Hail Mary, full of grace, the Lord is with you
Blessed are you among women,
And blest is the fruit of your womb, Jesus
Holy Mary, mother of God, pray for us sinners
Now and at the hour of our death, amen

Gentle woman, quiet light
Morning star so strong and bright
Gentle mother, peaceful dove
Teach us wisdom, teach us love

You were chosen by the Father
You were chosen for the Son
You were chosen from all women
And for woman, a shining one

Blessed are you among women
Blest in turn all women too
Blessed they with peaceful spirits
Blessed they with gentle hearts

Mary
by Liam Lawton

I have always imagined you to be young
With serene beauty
Sun-kissed face that searched the heavens
With questions only deep
Within your heart
With great love you carried your child
Watching Him grow beneath the moon of Israel
And under Egypt's stars

You took the splinters from His dusty hands
Turning wood on Joseph's bench
And held Him close when he spoke of things
You could only carry in your heart

Did you know what lay ahead?
How He would heal the sick
Raise the dead
Find the lost and
See the hungry fed?
Little children would be well again
The blind would see
Lazarus would rise
And the lame run free

Did you know that your heart would break?
When He was bound and beaten
Hung upon a tree

For all the world to see
The sin of humanity

Did your heart almost burst
When you heard the tomb was empty?
Did you run to see
And cry again so many tears
Of joy?
In Heaven you do not age
And you are forever young
You are beautiful
Because you love
May we know that love
In protection

In affection
In direction
Just as you watched over your own Son
Watch over us
Help us to find
That pure place in our heart
Beyond cynicism
Beyond hate
Beyond fear

Turn your gentle face towards us
That we might listen to your Cana words
"Do as He tells you"

May we walk one day
When life is done

Through the fields of paradise
Forever young
Enfolded in your mystery
O woman clothed in the sun

Miriam
by Pierce Pettis

No banners were unfurled
When God stepped into the world
Held in the arms of a little girl
Named Miriam
Who would ever believe
Your fiancé, your family
The teenage pregnancy
Of Miriam

But laws of nature were suspended
Death sentences rescinded
Throughout all the world
And all because of a little girl named Miriam

Medieval paintings glaring down
Stony figures judge and frown
Wearing a halo like a crown
Could that be Miriam

Gentile temples, stained glass swirls
Cherubim with golden curls
How unlike your Hebrew world
Miriam

I don't know how you ascended
I don't care what's been amended
There was one sure miracle
The faith of a little girl named Miriam

Oh you are blessed indeed
Blessed is the fruit of your tree
Yeshua kings of kings
And son of Miriam

No banners were unfurled
When God stepped into the world
Held in the arms of a little girl
Named Miriam

Marian Feast Days

January 1
Solemnity of Mary, Mother of God *

January 8
Our Lady of Prompt Succor

February 2
Presentation of the Lord

February 11
Our Lady of Lourdes

March 23
Our Lady of Victories

March 25
The Annunciation

May 1
Queen of Heaven

May 13
Our Lady of Fatima

May 31
The Visitation

June 8
Our Lady, Seat of Wisdom

June 27
Our Mother of Perpetual Help

July 16
Our Lady of Mount Carmel

August 15
The Assumption *

August 18
Coronation of Our Lady

August 22
The Queenship of Mary

August 26
Our Lady of Czestochowa

September 8
Birth of Mary

September 12
The Most Holy Name of Mary

September 15
Our Lady of Sorrows

Month of October
Month of the Rosary

October 7
Our Lady of the Rosary

November 21
Presentation of the Blessed Virgin Mary

December 8
Immaculate Conception *

December 12
Our Lady of Guadalupe

Holy Day of Obligation

The first Saturday of each month is dedicated to Marian devotions.

May is the Month of Mary.

October is the Month of the Rosary.

The Feast of the Immaculate Heart of Mary is the Saturday following the Second Sunday after Pentecost.

ALSO BY MATTHEW KELLY

The Rhythm of Life

Rediscover Jesus

Resisting Happiness

Rediscover Catholicism

Rediscover Lent

The Dream Manager

The Four Signs of a Dynamic Catholic

I Know Jesus

Perfectly Yourself

Why Am I Here?

The Seven Levels of Intimacy

Building Better Families

The One Thing

The Book of Courage

A Call to Joy

Mustard Seeds

Off Balance

The Long View

ABOUT THE AUTHOR

Matthew Kelly has dedicated his life to helping people and organizations become the-best-version-of-themselves! Born in Sydney, Australia, he began speaking and writing in his late teens while he was attending business school. Since that time, millions of people have attended his presentations in more than fifty countries.

Today Kelly is an internationally acclaimed speaker, author, and business consultant. His books have been published in more than twenty-five languages, have appeared on the *New York Times, Wall Street Journal,* and *USA Today* bestseller lists, and have sold more than twenty-five million copies.

He is the founder and owner of Floyd Consulting, a corporate consulting firm that specializes in increasing employee engagement. Floyd offers a number of training experiences for businesses of all sizes along with a variety of coaching opportunities.

Kelly is also the founder of Dynamic Catholic, a Cincinnati-based nonprofit organization that is redefining the way Catholics are inspired and educated. Dynamic Catholic's mission is to re-energize the Catholic Church in America.

In a time when traditional publishing is in transition and turmoil, he is also passionate about giving other authors a chance to pursue their dreams. He accomplishes this as the founder and CEO of Beacon Publishing.

His personal interests include golf, piano, literature, spirituality, and spending time with his family and friends.